Investing in Cannabis

Investing in Cannabis

The Next Great Investment Opportunity

Dan Ahrens

For general information on our other products and services or for technical support, please contact our Customer Care Department within the United States at (800) 762-2974, outside the United States at (317) 572-3993, or fax (317) 572-4002.

Wiley publishes in a variety of print and electronic formats and by print-on-demand. Some material included with standard print versions of this book may not be included in e-books or in print-on-demand. If this book refers to media such as a CD or DVD that is not included in the version you purchased, you may download this material at http://booksupport.wiley.com. For more information about Wiley products, visit www.wiley.com.

Library of Congress Cataloging-in-Publication Data

Names: Ahrens, Dan, author.
Title: Investing in cannabis : the next great investment opportunity / Dan Ahrens.
Description: First edition. | Hoboken, New Jersey : John Wiley & Sons, Inc., [2021] | Includes index.
Identifiers: LCCN 2020034694 (print) | LCCN 2020034695 (ebook) | ISBN 9781119691013 (hardback) | ISBN 9781119691006 (adobe pdf) | ISBN 9781119690993 (epub)
Subjects: LCSH: Marijuana industry. | Cannabis–Economic aspects. | Marijuana–Economic aspects. | Investments.
Classification: LCC HD9019.M38 A47 2021 (print) | LCC HD9019.M38 (ebook) | DDC 338.4/763379–dc23
LC record available at https://lccn.loc.gov/2020034694
LC ebook record available at https://lccn.loc.gov/2020034695

Cover Design: Paul McCarthy
Cover Art: © Getty Images | Lalita Chaudhari / Eyeem

Printed in the United States of America.

SKY10021331_092220

Contents

A Note to Readers   vii

Preface   ix

Acknowledgments   xi

Chapter 1: Like Investing in Alcohol at the End of Prohibition   1

Chapter 2: The Feds, the DEA, and the War on Drugs   13

Chapter 3: The Cannabis Investment Opportunity   21

Chapter 4: Buy Low, Sell High?   29

Chapter 5: The Movement Toward Legality   45

Chapter 6: Canada Versus the United States   65

Chapter 7: The State of the States   75

Chapter 8: The Worldwide Opportunity   95

Chapter 9: Canadian Licensed Producers   97

Chapter 10: US Multi-state Operators   117

Chapter 11: Extraction and Concentrates   135

Chapter 12: Hemp and CBD Focused 141

Chapter 13: Pharmaceutical and Biotech 149

Chapter 14: Suppliers and Everyone Else 159

Chapter 15: Mergers and Acquisitions 169

Chapter 16: Don't Get Burned 175

Appendix I: Portfolio Manager Dan Ahrens' Cannabis
Exchange-traded Fund Holdings on June 30, 2020 183

Appendix II: Portfolio Manager Dan Ahrens' US Cannabis
Exchange-traded Fund Planned Holdings in August 2020 185

Appendix III: Constituents of the North American Marijuana
Index as of June 30, 2020 187

About the Author 189

Index 191

A Note to Readers

The opinions expressed in this book are those of the author alone, not the publisher, and not necessarily those of AdvisorShares Investments, LLC, AdvisorShares Trust, the AdvisorShares Pure Cannabis ETF (NYSE: YOLO), or the Advisor-Shares Pure US Cannabis ETF (NYSE: MSOS). Opinions are subject to change, are not guaranteed, and should not be considered a recommendation to buy or sell any security or AdvisorShares Fund. There are risks involved in investing in evolving industries that may be adversely affected by legislative initiatives as well as changes in social and economic conditions, all of which may impact the profitability of companies.

Preface

A book about investing in cannabis was not even possible just a few short years ago. There wasn't enough to invest in! Publicly traded and exchange-listed cannabis stocks have exploded onto the scene with legalization in Canada and a constantly growing list of locations in the United States. Cannabis includes both medical and recreational adult-use marijuana, but also hemp-based CBD (cannabidiol) and other cannabinoids with a long list of potential uses. Pharmaceutical and biotech companies are just scratching the surface of cannabis-based applications. Marijuana dispensaries are quickly opening all around the United States, Canada, and in countries across the globe. Cannabis based products are everywhere – lotions, oils, beverages, food – wellness products of all types for humans and for pets.

This book will focus of investing in cannabis through publicly traded stocks that are available to everyone. The opportunity is substantial. The new business of cannabis will have great success stories but will also have abysmal failures. As a new industry, the ups and downs will be extreme. A lot of companies won't make it. Some may be downright fraudulent. We will discuss the state of legalization and name the top cannabis operators in the United States and Canada, in biotech and pharmaceuticals, CBD, and all the other associated businesses. I'll tell you what to look for, and what to avoid.

Acknowledgments

T his book and our cannabis funds would not have been possible without contributions from a great number of people. I would like to thank AdvisorShares CEO Noah Hamman for his ideas and for his drive to get the first cannabis focused, actively managed, exchange-traded fund launched in the United States. And to everyone else at AdvisorShares, thanks for all you do. Managing Director of Distribution James Carl helped with some great data and charts. Thanks to Lynn Brautigan and Mackenzie Peterson in our marketing department for all their constant work on content. Lynn created some nice-looking charts for the book. Investment Consultant Lance Davidson – keep up the great communications. Thanks to our Chief Compliance Officer Stefanie Little. And thank you to Ryan Graham, a Vice President at JConnelly PR, for your good work with the press.

For the launch of my firm's cannabis-related funds, a great many people at partner firms and servicing firms were involved. There are too many to name but include people at trading firms, swap dealers, market makers, authorized participants, legal firms, tax and audit, and of course the fund distributor, fund administrator, and the stock exchange.

All of the people in various groups at Bank of New York Mellon and BNY Mellon Asset Servicing for Exchange Traded Funds have been great to work with. We've been fund clients of BNY Mellon for more than 10 years and brainstormed with them about cannabis stocks for well over a year before launching our fund. I appreciate their understanding of what's legal and what's not, and how to handle our cannabis investments properly.

The Exchange Traded Products team at the New York Stock Exchange have been great partners and helped us launch dozens of funds quickly and efficiently. They've also helped us get some great ticker symbols.

Our outside counsel at Morgan, Lewis & Bockius LLP have represented AdvisorShares since our founding and always aided us in being an innovative fund company. They are the best in the business of exchange-traded funds.

The team in Global Securities Finance at Cowen Execution Services LLC / Cowen and Company LLC have been instrumental in our fund's investment process and in our access to the US multi-state operators we invest in. Cowen has been an essential firm in North American cannabis expansion.

Thanks to Kevin Harreld, senior acquisitions editor at John Wiley & Sons, for seeking me out and for support all along the way.

Thanks to my beautiful wife, Lana Ahrens. Forced to read a few of the early chapters in development, she claimed that she actually found the book interesting. Owen Ahrens and Arden Ahrens – thank you for being born and for being generally great kids. Keep making those good grades in school.

Chapter 1
Like Investing in Alcohol at the End of Prohibition

"Prohibition has made nothing but trouble."

—Al Capone

O n December 5, 1933, at 3:32 p.m. local time, Utah became the 36th state (the required three-quarters of the 48 states) to ratify the Twenty-First Amendment to the United States Constitution. Prohibition ended. Only 16 years earlier in 1917, the Eighteenth Amendment had been proposed in Congress to establish a ban on the manufacture, transportation, and sale of "intoxication liquors" in the United States. Circumstances made Prohibition a failure, and the Eighteenth Amendment was the first Constitutional amendment in the history of the United States of America to be repealed. The primary reason – money.

The 1920s (the roaring twenties) were a boom time for the US economy. Life was good. Following victory in World War I, the United States was becoming a true world power. New consumer goods spread into households with the advent of mass production, and the modern automobile and airline industries were born. The US financial system was thriving without the legal sale of alcohol. But the Eighteenth Amendment had actually done little to curb the sale and consumption of liquor. It was simply transported

1

and sold illegally. It was done with a wink and a nod among many Americans. The Volstead Act (formally named the National Prohibition Act) was a law that became effective on January 17, 1920, to provide enforcement for the Eighteenth Amendment. It created a special enforcement unit of the Treasury Department (Bureau of Prohibition), and formally began Prohibition. For the wealthier, more powerful, or simply "connected" individuals among American society, drinking came easy. It almost turned into a game of enjoying smuggled alcohol and visiting speakeasies. In another interesting side effect of Prohibition, increasingly strong distilled spirits surged in popularity. The appeal of beer and wine was diminished. Distilled spirits were more profitable to produce, cheaper to transport, and easier to smuggle into the country.

Despite policing efforts of the Treasury Department and other law-enforcement agencies, organized crime reaped the real benefits of the illegal alcohol trade. Organized crime flourished. Organized crime became more organized. With America enjoying good fortune in the twenties, many people weren't concerned with crime – especially crime involving alcohol. Gangsters often became glorified celebrities. Everything was fine until the economy suddenly and violently came crashing down. America's Great Depression began with the Black Thursday stock market crash of October 24, 1929. The Great Depression happened for a host of reasons. The stock market crash followed a period of gross overconfidence and overproduction of goods. A panic in the stock market sparked a panic at the banks. A weak banking system allowed banks to fail and close. Bankruptcies and job losses snowballed.

While the United States was navigating through the Depression, the federal government desperately needed revenue if it were to help set the economy on a correct path and put jobless Americans back to work. Federal income taxes had only been created a few years earlier with the Sixteenth Amendment of 1913. It was a major shift in the federal government's revenue system. Prior to creation of the income tax, alcohol taxes had generated as much as 40% of the federal government budget. With Prohibition, the government had quickly become incredibly dependent on income tax as its primary revenue source. The Depression changed that. Incomes suffered and income taxes suffered. Income tax revenue dropped 60% from 1930 to 1933. The legalization and taxation of alcoholic beverages was an easy target. In the 1932 presidential election, the Governor of New York, Democrat Franklin D. Roosevelt (FDR) campaigned against the financial failures of President Herbert Hoover's administration. The repeal of Prohibition was an important part of Roosevelt's Democratic Party platform. He easily defeated the incumbent Hoover in a landslide victory on Tuesday, November 8, 1932. Just three months later in February of 1933, Congress would propose the Twenty-First Amendment to repeal Prohibition.

The end of Prohibition was a major financial victory for the federal government. Millions of dollars collected in alcohol taxes helped to finance President Roosevelt's New Deal programs in the years that followed. Alcohol helped to financially heal the country as it slowly recovered from the worldwide economic crisis – the most severe in the history of the industrialized world.

Any long-term investor putting money in a diversified group of alcohol stocks near the end of Prohibition would do very, very well. The performance numbers from 1933, or anywhere around that time, up to the present day, are rather remarkable.

Time to Buy

Using US publicly traded stock price data from the well-known and publicly available CRSP (Center for Research in Security Prices) library of Dr. Kenneth French, Tuck School of Business at Dartmouth College, we looked at the exchange-listed securities of the US stock market broken down into 30 industry portfolios. Among a myriad of available data points for stock prices and dividends going back to 1926, the database provides monthly investment returns for each industry grouping. We chose to begin in 1933 – the year that Prohibition was repealed in the United States. We're certainly not the first to study this industry data. Numerous case studies have been completed and articles have been written using various timeframes and methods for crunching the data. The results are the same. From the lows of the Great Depression, alcohol stocks outperformed the other industries and outperformed the general market.

Beer and alcohol total return of $10,000

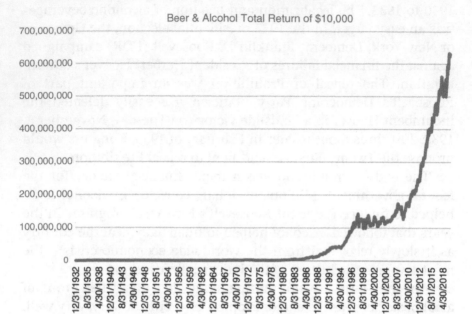

Beer & Alcohol Total Return of $10,000

Source: AdvisorShares, based on data from the CRSP library of
Dr. Kenneth French, December 31, 1932, to December 31, 2019

Admittedly – compounded investment performance over a long
period of time (like more than 85 years) can cause a very exaggerated
graph. The early years of a long-term compound return chart usually
look almost flat. The stock performance of alcohol in the 1930s was
anything but flat. It was extremely volatile. But the fact remains that
since 1933 alcohol stocks have outperformed other industries such
as chemicals, communications, construction, financials, healthcare,
oil, and retail. As we started our calculations in 1933, annualized
industry performance numbers may look better than expected, but
please remember that we're calculating from a seriously low point in
the years following the stock market crash in 1929. Another industry
performed almost as well as alcohol. It was tobacco. If you're thinking of similarities to marijuana or cannabis, you're right. But there
is much more to follow.

30 industries listed in the CRSP library, annualized
performance December 31, 1932, through December 31, 2019

Industry	%
Automobiles and Trucks	11.00
Beer and Alcohol	**13.54**
Printing and Publishing	9.45
Business Equipment	12.87
Aircraft, Ships, and Railroad Equipment	12.89
Chemicals	11.27
Apparel	11.13
Construction and Construction Materials	10.99
Coal	7.82
Electrical Equipment	12.54
Fabricated Products and Machinery	11.75
Banking, Insurance, Real Estate, Trading	11.65
Food Products	11.85
Recreation	12.57
Healthcare, Medical Equipment, Pharmaceutical Products	12.67
Consumer Goods	11.53
Restaurants, Hotels, Motels	12.66
Precious Metals, non-Metallic, and Industrial Metal Mining	9.02
Petroleum and Natural Gas	11.80
Everything Else: Sanitary, A/C, Irrigation, Cogen	9.46
Business Supplies and Shipping Containers	11.45
Retail	12.48
Personal and Business Services	12.92
Tobacco Products	**13.13**
Steel Works	8.64
Communication	9.97
Transportation	10.41
Textiles	10.69
Utilities	9.60
Wholesale	12.06

Source: Performance calculated by AdvisorShares Investments, LLC. Average value
weighted returns from monthly performance data from the CRSP library of
Dr. Kenneth French.

In October of 2018, an article was published by *Barron's,* "What Alcohol Stocks During Prohibition Say About Marijuana Stocks Today," by Al Root. The article's main point was that the value of alcohol stocks dropped after Prohibition was lifted. While factually correct, I feel the premise of the article was all wrong. The article was pointing out that alcohol stocks were a lousy investment in the year that followed the end of Prohibition. Alcohol didn't automatedly go up beginning on December 5, 1933. What the article failed to mention was that alcohol stocks had already gone up more than 350% following Franklin D. Roosevelt's (FDR's) presidential victory in November of 1932 and the Twenty-First Amendment being proposed in Congress in February of 1933.

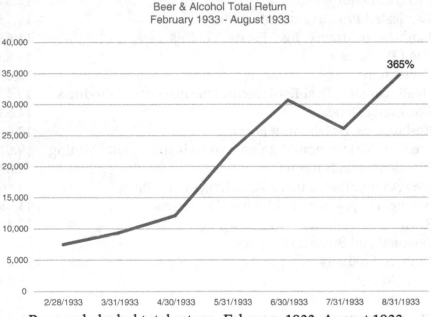

Beer and alcohol total return, February 1933–August 1933
Source: AdvisorShares, based on data from the CRSP library of
Dr. Kenneth French.

While alcohol's manufacture and sale had "only" been illegal for 14 years, it was once again a new industry in the United States that required hard work to recreate operations and infrastructure – and to replace the alcohol black market that had been operating since 1920. Extreme stock price volatility followed.

From a high point in August of 1933 to a temporary low around July of 1934, alcohol stocks as a group dropped almost 50% in value. As the *Barron's* article described – a poor investment.

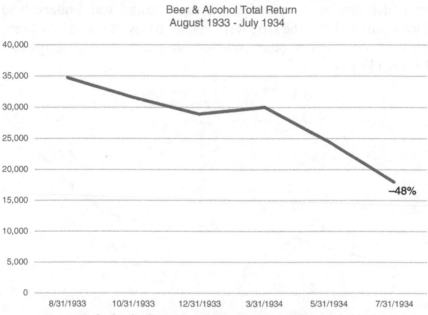

Beer and alcohol total return, August 1933–July 1934
Source: AdvisorShares, based on data from the CRSP library of Dr. Kenneth French.

When investing, it's very important to understand the psychology of investing. What makes a stock go up or down? More than anything, it's about supply and demand. When investors have demand for a stock, that demand means there's more buyers than sellers. There's buying pressure. The stock price goes up. I'm pointing this out now because in June or July of 1934 there wasn't any buying pressure on alcohol stocks. After a great run-up following FDR's victory and in anticipation of Prohibition coming to an end, alcohol stocks turned terrible again. Investors were sellers. Alcohol stocks went down in almost every month over an 11-month period. Some investors may have been selling to lock in their gains from the previous year. Other investors probably thought they were too late and had missed the boat on investing in alcohol stocks.

By October of 1935, alcohol stocks gained almost 100% from the lows in the summer of 1934. What changed? I don't know. Some wise investors must have decided that alcohol was undervalued once again and had the long-term vision to buy at low prices. Once stock prices reversed, other investors joined in. Plenty of ups and downs followed.

Beer and alcohol total return, July 1934–October 1935
Source: AdvisorShares, based on data from the CRSP library of Dr. Kenneth French.

Through truly extreme volatility at the end of alcohol's Prohibition, even the years 1933 through 1935 provided terrific investment performance to early investors.

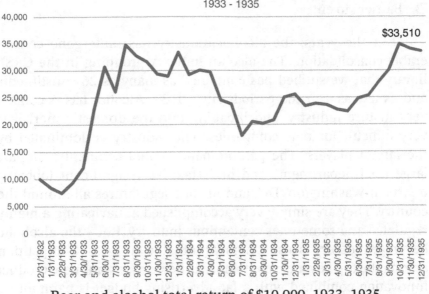

Beer and alcohol total return of $10,000, 1933–1935
Source: AdvisorShares, based on data from the CRSP library of Dr. Kenneth French.

While the alcohol industry in the 1930s was highly volatile, in the decades that followed it turned into one of the steadiest, most predictable industries around. The alcohol business is often referred to as recession-proof. People are going to drink no matter what's going on with the economy – no matter what's going on with the stock market. People don't stop drinking when the stock market drops. They may even drink more! The spread of coronavirus (COVID-19) in 2020 isolated people at home and caused a definite spike in alcohol sales across the board. In the longer term, when the economy slows or the overall stock market dips, investors traditionally shift to safer, more predictable investment sectors such as consumer staples – and alcohol.

The health of the alcoholic beverage industry is distinguished by three major characteristics:

1. Concentration

2. Profitability
3. Barriers to entry

Over the years, the alcohol industry has undergone considerable consolidation. The alcohol industry grouping in the CRSP library that we studied has contained as many as 26 constituents and as few as 4 in the periods since 1933. Alcohol has become a very mature industry, and breaking into the domestic market is very difficult for new companies. The industry is dominated by the largest players. The predominant alcohol companies employ large legal departments and undertake very significant lobbying efforts in Washington, DC, and in state legislatures all around the country. They are simply very accomplished at navigating a highly regulated and sometimes contentious industry. But – the alcoholic beverage industry is also a highly profitable business. Competition among the top beverage companies is fierce. Constant new product innovation combined with a fat advertising budget is paramount. The best companies have dominant distribution networks and are masters of promotion.

People may drink alcohol no matter what's going on in the world, but they don't always drink the same thing. In the United States and around the world, shifts in alcoholic beverage sales are caused by changing tastes, demographics, and disposable incomes. Along with rising incomes and a strong economy come sales of fine wines and high-end spirits. Mass-produced lower-end beers have been on a slow decline. Craft beers and, more recently, craft liquors have been on an upswing. Smaller startups in craft beer, small production wines, and designer distilled beverages are often targeted for acquisition by their bigger competitors.

All of this brings me back to cannabis. In some circles, cannabis has been called a long-term risk to the alcohol industry. Top alcoholic beverage companies have even expressed concern in annual reports and investor conference calls about cannabis legalization cutting into alcohol sales. In a paper published in early 2018 and cited in numerous publications, researchers at three universities described a joint study covering a 10-year period in US counties with legalized cannabis sales. They claimed a 13.8% drop in beer sales following the legalization of marijuana. The study showed considerable overlap in the consumer base for legal marijuana smokers and beer drinkers. Overall, data showed that sales of alcohol were 15% lower on average in states with legalized marijuana. But another study showed just the opposite. A January 2019 report from the Distilled Spirits Counsel, and quoted in *Forbes* and other major outlets, stated that "there is no evidence that legalization has had any impact on spirits sales, nor is there any evidence that it has impacted total alcohol sales." They studied the three states with the longest history of legalized recreational marijuana sales: Colorado, Washington, and Oregon. Per capita spirits sales actually increased since recreational marijuana legalization went into effect in each state. Wine sales were mixed – up in two states, down in the other. Per capita beer sales declined in all three states, but consistent with the national trend in beer sales and not isolated to just these three states. It is interesting that supposedly scientific studies can vary so much depending on who's doing the study.

Regardless of whether cannabis legalization has any real impact on alcohol sales, savvy beverage companies are quickly jumping into the cannabis business. Cannabis companies and beverage makers are both investing heavily in the potential market for cannabis-based adult beverages.

Big beer company Heineken launched Hi-Fi Hops, a cannabis-only beverage available in California dispensaries under its Lagunitas brand. It tastes like beer but contains no alcohol. The world's largest brewer, Anheuser-Busch InBev, and a large public Canadian cannabis company are in a joint venture to produce cannabis-infused beverages. Canadian American brewer Molson Coors is in another. Diversified alcoholic beverage giant Constellation Brands invested over $4 billion in 2018 for a 38% ownership stake in Canada's largest marijuana company. Canadian cannabis beverages just began to hit store shelves for the first time at the very end of 2019 – and in limited amounts. Beverage production and sales are expected to explode through 2020 and 2021. The cannabis beverage market alone is expected to be worth billions in the United States and Canada by 2022. But that is just one very small piece of the potential for total cannabis sales.

Will the overall cannabis business of the future look much like the alcoholic beverage business of past decades? Highly profitable. Concentrated. Innovative. Influential. Recession-proof? Time will tell.

Chapter 2
The Feds, the DEA, and the War on Drugs

"Drugs are bad."

– Mr. Mackey, South Park Elementary

The legalization of cannabis may present an amazing investment opportunity. But wait. Why is cannabis illegal in the first place? Most people just assume that marijuana or cannabis has always been illegal. It's a drug. Drugs are bad. But it's not as simple as that. Marijuana's criminalization is a convoluted story full of money, politics, racism – and conspiracy theories.

Federal level marijuana prohibition began just a few short years after alcohol prohibition was repealed. The Marihuana Tax Act of 1937 used an excise tax on all sales of hemp to effectively make possession or sale of marihuana illegal throughout the United States. (Notice that it was spelled with an "h"). Government sentiment against narcotic and other drug use began in the late 1800s and gained steam through the early 1900s.

Before it was made illegal, cannabis had been used in the Americas for hundreds of years. Land-owning American colonists of Jamestown, Virginia were expected to grow and export hemp plants to support their benefactors in England. George Washington grew hemp at Mount Vernon as one of his primary crops. Thomas

Jefferson also grew hemp, as did many farmers of the day. Hemp was used as rope, fabric, and even a fuel source. In 1799, Napoleon brought other strains of cannabis from Egypt to France, and Europe began to learn of the medicinal qualities of cannabis. By the 1840s and 1850s, cannabis extracts and tinctures were going mainstream in American and European pharmacies as a treatment for countless maladies. Separately, smoking hash was thought of as a fashionable and exotic habit among middle- and upper-class society. Hundreds of hashish parlors emerged in New York and other east coast cities. But the word marijuana or "marihuana" was little known to most Americans.

Which brings us to the supposed conspiracy to exterminate the hemp and cannabis business leading up to the Marihuana Tax Act of 1937. Our characters are newspaperman William Randolph Hearst, the Du Pont family and their DuPont chemical company, Andrew Mellon and Mellon Bank, and Mellon's relative by marriage, Harry Anslinger.

Hearst was the most powerful media mogul of the time. His vast array of newspapers and magazines were the most read nationwide. As a newspaper man, he was supposedly heavily invested in the timber industry for the development of paper products. Dupont was the maker of synthetic materials and had just invested nylon in 1927. Nylon could revolutionize the textile industry and begin to replace the use of natural fibers. Andrew Mellon was the nation's richest man when he was appointed Secretary of the Treasury in 1921. Mellon Bank was one of the most powerful financial institutions in the world, and Mellon Bank was also the financial backer for DuPont.

In 1930, as Secretary of the Treasury under his third president, Andrew Mellon was in position to appoint the founding commissioner to the Treasury's new Federal Bureau of Narcotics (FBN). He appointed Harry J. Anslinger. Mellon was uncle to Anslinger's wife. Remember that the Treasury Department was also the main enforcer for Prohibition. With the loss of alcohol prohibition as one of the Treasury's main functions just a couple years later, it's thought that Mellon and Anslinger needed a new illegal substance to focus efforts and budgets on. That new focus was squarely on marijuana.

Anslinger needed to justify his bureau's very existence. The Commissioner of the FBN became a very aggressive and outspoken critic of marijuana usage.

With Harry Anslinger fighting a war on drugs (before that term existed), others ostensibly joined in to demonize marijuana use. The rich newspaper baron Hearst used his influential portfolio of newspapers and magazines to sway public opinion on the evils of the mind-altering marijuana plant. Advertisements and articles pointed to the rise of crime, violence, and purported "sexual deviance" with marijuana use. Rhetoric from Anslinger, Hearst and other anti-drug propagandists primarily targeted non-white and lower-class communities. Extreme racism and class warfare ran rampant.

There's conflicting information about where the term marijuana even originated. US immigration from Mexico surged between 1910 and 1920 with individuals wanting to escape the violence of the Mexican Revolution. It's believed that Mexican immigrants in the southwest brought casual smoking of the marijuana plant along with them. We don't know if the word was spelled "marihuana" in government documents purposefully or by accident. We do believe that those looking to undermine marijuana chose a word that was foreign to most Americans and as a way to connect it to immigrants and minorities while dissociating it from socially acceptable hemp or medical cannabis.

While Hearst and Anslinger campaigned against marijuana on what they claimed were moral grounds, other conspirators possessed financial interests. The US tobacco industry was booming. Marijuana leaf could be a competitor. DuPont's nylon and other new synthetics could excel with hemp out of the picture. It's also alleged that Randolph Hearst and the timber industry feared the potential growth of hemp-based paper products.

It was Federal Bureau of Narcotics commissioner Harry Anslinger who drafted and lobbied for enactment of the Marihuana Tax Act of 1937.

While this all makes for a good conspiracy theory that's been circulated by cannabis proponents, it is just that – a conspiracy theory. In the early twentieth century hemp was a rather insignificant crop.

While clothing can be made from hemp fibers, cotton had already proven itself to be much more practical and the cotton gin had revolutionized that industry many years prior. Just as hemp wasn't a cotton competitor, it was not a real competitor to DuPont's new synthetic nylon. Hemp can also be used to produce high-quality paper, but by 1937, hemp planting had managed to grow to only 14,000 total acres in the United States. Compared to hundreds of millions of acres of timber and about 10 million acres of cotton, hemp's share of the market was totally insignificant.

On the other hand, racism, fear, and anti-drug zealotism were the real reasons behind marijuana's criminalization. Its outlaw was pursued by many of the same extremists behind Prohibition. It also gave Andrew Mellon's Treasury Department and Harry Anslinger's Federal Bureau of Narcotics something to do.

City and state laws had been passed making cannabis illegal decades before our Marihuana Tax Act of 1937. California had banned non-prescription cannabis in 1913. New York City did in 1914. Through the remainder of the decade and into the 1920s, other states and municipalities quickly followed suit. Unfortunately, it's said that enforcement of these new laws was targeted almost entirely against Mexican and black communities. By the end of 1936, all 48 states had formed laws to ban or regulate marijuana on some level.

While illegal marijuana use was being policed, its minor use as a medicine was also in decline. The development of aspirin, morphine, and other modern drugs replaced marijuana in the treatment of pain and other medical conditions. The new federal marijuana law was structured in a fashion like several other Acts of the time – attacking the issue financially. The Marihuana Tax Act of 1937 maintained the right to use marijuana for medicinal purposes but required pharmacists and physicians who prescribed the drug to register with federal authorities and pay an annual tax. The 1937 Act simply made legal marijuana use prohibitively expensive. Prescriptions of marijuana dramatically declined as doctors generally chose to avoid the unnecessary hassles and costs.

The Marihuana Tax Act of 1937 was ruled unconstitutional by the United States Supreme Court in 1969 and overturned. You can thank famous psychedelic drug advocate and Harvard psychologist Timothy Leary for that. As Leary faced a 30-year prison sentence for marijuana possession, he hired a powerful team of lawyers to defend him. His attorneys argued that the Tax Act violated his Fifth Amendment rights because he had to tell federal authorities he possessed pot so they could tax it. The Supreme Court agreed.

The federal government followed up with the Controlled Substance Act (CSA) in 1970, which established the modern prohibition against marijuana. Marijuana was lumped in as a "Schedule I" drug along with the other drugs purported to be the most dangerous, like heroin and LSD.

According to the United States Drug Enforcement Agency website, drugs are classified into five distinct categories (or schedules) depending on the drug's acceptable medical use and the drug's abuse or dependency potential. Schedule I drugs have a high potential for abuse and the potential to create severe psychological and/or physical dependence. Schedule I drugs, substances, or chemicals are also defined as drugs with no currently accepted medical use. As the CSA was written, Schedule V drugs represented the least potential for abuse. This 1970 Schedule I listing of marijuana in the CSA and enforced by the DEA would hamper the cannabis industry for decades to come. By comparison, even cocaine and methamphetamine are listed as Schedule II drugs in the CSA Schedule. Still dangerous and with a high potential for abuse, but theoretically lesser than that of marijuana. Ridiculous.

It's been said that Nixon himself wanted marijuana placed as a Schedule I drug, although just temporarily and pending review by a commission that he appointed. The commission's report recommending decriminalization for the possession and distribution of marijuana for personal use would be ignored. It's rumored that much of Nixon's early seventies' anti-drug push was more about squashing political dissent, social upheaval, and young, liberal anti-war rebellion than it was about any dangers of drug use itself. And much like with the Marihuana Tax Act of 1937, its thought that a heavy dose of racism against minorities was mixed in as well.

The "War on Drugs" began in earnest around June of 1971 when President Nixon named drug abuse to be "public enemy number one" and increased federal funding for drug-control agencies and drug-treatment programs. In 1973 the Drug Enforcement Agency (DEA) was created to consolidate all federal efforts toward the fight against drug abuse.

Marijuana's most restrictive Schedule I class severely hinders most scientific and pharmaceutical research. The scheduling itself prevents research that could show marijuana's medical efficacy and safety. Researchers in the United States face daunting regulatory hurdles to the study of any Schedule I drug with an overly cumbersome approval process at the DEA and with the Food and Drug Administration (FDA). Marijuana is the only Schedule I drug that the DEA prohibits from being produced by private laboratories for scientific research.

Between the Schedule I designation, the 1970 Bank Secrecy Act (BSA), and other federal laws, virtually all banking associated with the cannabis business is illegal. With marijuana illegal at a US federal level, banks and other financial institutions insured by federal agencies are forced to fully avoid cannabis companies – even those operating as medical marijuana companies or otherwise operating legally under state law. Banks could face severe criminal or financial penalties for even offering the most basic banking services to the marijuana industry.

Even following the Nixon regime, the Drug Enforcement Agency was a comparatively insignificant piece of overall federal law enforcement efforts until Ronald Reagan's presidency began in 1981. Reagan greatly expanded the scope and reach of the drug war with a strong focus on criminal punishment over drug treatment. Reagan's programs led to a massive increase in nationwide incarcerations for nonviolent drug offenses, while First Lady Nancy Reagan pushed her highly publicized "Just Say No" anti-drug campaign.

As a result of the new 1980s' drug crackdown, cannabis companies in the United States operating legally under any state level law are exposed to Section 280E of the US tax code. Just as the old Marihuana Tax Act of 1937 targeted drugs financially, Internal Revenue Code Section 280E was implemented during Reagan's presidency to keep drug dealers from writing off business expenses from federal income taxes. Section 280E forbids any business that sells a federally illicit substance from taking normal corporate income tax deductions. State legal cannabis companies in the United States are paying higher than normal effective tax rates.

Public support for the war on drugs has obviously declined in recent times. Societal changes have led to a more tolerant view on recreational drug use. While the war on drugs is still technically being waged, it is done at a much less intense level than it was during its peak in the 1980s. The war on drugs campaign has been ineffective. Most feel that it has led to racial divide with an acknowledgment of the wide disparity in punishments imposed. Reforms have been enacted but have a long way to go. According to the Pew Research Center, between 2009 and 2013, at least 40 states took steps to soften drug laws. Many states have lowered penalties and shortened mandatory minimum sentences.

While marijuana's DEA, banking issues, and federal law remain in place for now, there exists an awfully large amount of illegal marijuana sales that could be replaced with legal, taxable marijuana sales – with time and with proper legislation.

Chapter 3
The Cannabis Investment Opportunity

"A friend with weed is a friend indeed."

– Pops O'Donnell

C annabis may be comparable to alcohol in many ways, but it also has much, much more to offer. Cannabis isn't even a defined "industry" by today's standards. Cannabis-related companies fall into all sorts of categories, including agriculture, retail, pharmaceuticals, biotechnology, healthcare, household products, and even real estate investments trusts (REITS) or other investment companies.

I've heard negative arguments that marijuana is just a commodity that can be grown at home. Of course, it is possible to grow at home. But most normal adults aren't going to the trouble. I had a friend in college that turned his walk-in closet into an in-home weed grow. That's not a very adult thing to do. You can also brew beer at home. Not many people do. It's a nice hobby, but hardly a multibillion-dollar industry. You can even distill your own liquor at home. But the distilled beverage industry isn't concerned with people making home moonshine.

Even as a major industry, we still hear that marijuana is "just a crop" to be farmed and then traded like wheat, corn, or any other commodity. It's a silly argument. Wheat, barley, corn, potatoes? While farming is its own multibillion-dollar industry and the world's population largely depends on the crops for our very existence – it's not a great investment opportunity for individuals. But fine bourbon made from corn? Beer from wheat and barley? Vodka from potatoes? Rum from sugar cane? All very profitable products and an excellent investment opportunity for the past 85 years. The wine industry isn't just about growing grapes. The tobacco industry certainly isn't just about growing leaf tobacco. Big Tobacco has been wildly profitable for decades (even while smoking rates continue to decline) because cigarettes have outrageously high profit margins. Cigarette profit margins are easily the highest among all consumer products, even after a huge piece of the pie goes to the government in taxes.

Cannabis isn't just a plant. It is a plant, but also a finished flower product that can be sold at a huge profit margin per pound. It is an ingredient to be used in foods, beverages, oils, and lotions. It's also a long list of cannabinoid compounds with medical usage just in the early stages of discovery. Whatever you call it, cannabis, marijuana, hemp, CBD, and all the other cannabinoids in various forms have many uses and applications.

In addition to the obvious market for legal recreational use – marijuana, medical use marijuana, edibles, topicals, oils, and vapes – cannabis expansion can impact a multitude of industries.

- **Alcohol:** Much of the alcohol industry is concerned with legal marijuana cutting into market share. Some of the largest companies in the alcohol industry have already made significant investments to the marijuana business or entered joint ventures. Cannabis-infused alcoholic beverages are hitting the market, and many more are expected.
- **Non-alcoholic Beverages:** Marijuana-infused and CBD non-alcoholic beverages are quickly coming to market as competition to coffee drinks and sodas while being promoted as healthier alternatives.

- **Tobacco:** Much like the alcohol industry, Big Tobacco has concerns of marijuana cutting into sales. Cigarette sales have been shrinking for years. For many tobacco users, marijuana will emerge as a recreational substitute for cigarettes. Like alcohol, tobacco companies are joining in the cannabis business.
- **Construction and Real Estate:** Marijuana cultivation is a highly specialized business and will lead to increased demand for real estate and specialized facilities. Real estate investment trusts (REITS) can play an important role in providing land, greenhouses, and warehouse facilities.
- **E-commerce:** Online marketing and sales for cannabis-related products are expected to skyrocket. Much of the potential e-commerce market is suppressed by law, but online sales should flourish with regulatory change. Many consumers that may not be comfortable in a cannabis dispensary will gladly complete transactions with internet retailers.
- **Pharmaceutical:** Big pharma is barely beginning to conduct research into the full uses of delta-9-tetrahydrocannabinol (THC), cannabidiol (CBD), and other cannabis-derived cannabinoids in the development of drugs. Much of the industry has been handcuffed by burdensome regulation over marijuana as an illicit drug and preventing valid scientific study.
- **Pet Products:** Sales of CBD treats, oils, and other additives are growing rapidly as cannabinoids are promoted for pet vitality and calming.
- **Health, Wellness and Beauty:** Cannabis derived oils, lotions, and other topicals are being introduced to a wide spectrum of beauty and wellness applications.
- **Cannabis Tourism:** Cannabis tourism is a thing! Marijuana cultivation and production facilities have become new attractions for tourists, much like winery or brewery tours for a different kind of consumer.

Cannabis Primer

- Cannabis, also known as marijuana, is an annual flowering plant from the family Cannabaceae, which is native to Central Asia and the Indian subcontinent. The plant has psychoactive (mind-altering) properties and is used for industrial, recreational, and medical purposes. Cannabis is made up of more than 100 unique chemical compounds, known as cannabinoids. Although the effects of all cannabinoids on the human body are not clearly established, the two most common and well-known cannabinoids are delta-9-tetrahydrocannabinol (THC) and cannabidiol (CBD).

- THC is the main mind-altering ingredient found in the cannabis plant and is the chemical responsible for most of marijuana's psychological effects. It acts like the cannabinoid chemicals made naturally by the human body. Cannabinoid receptors are part of the endocannabinoid system, which is involved in a variety of physiological processes including appetite, pain sensation, mood, and memory. According to the National Institute on Drug Abuse (NIDA), THC attaches to these receptors and activates them and affects a person's memory, pleasure, movements, thinking, concentration, coordination, and sensory and time perception. THC stimulates cells in the brain to release dopamine, thus creating euphoria (the "high").

- CBD, on the other hand, is a non-psychoactive cannabinoid and binds very weakly, if at all, to CB1 receptors. Instead, it has medicinal properties that are used to help reduce inflammation and ease pain. It also is used to treat stress, depression, and anxiety, and to combat cancer, epilepsy, schizophrenia, multiple sclerosis, migraines, arthritis, and the side effects of cancer treatments. The positive medicinal effects make CBD-heavy strains of cannabis a popular choice for use among patients. Other cannabinoids such as cannabichromene (CBC), cannabigerol (CBG), and cannabinol (CBN) also have displayed similar therapeutic properties and are likely to be used for medicinal purposes once research validates their efficacy in treating medical conditions.

Source: Intro-Blue.

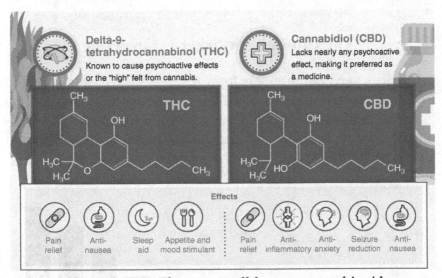

THC and CBD: The most well-known cannabinoids
Source: Intro-Blue, Visual Capitalist.

Natural cannabinoid compounds are unique to the cannabis plant. There have been at least 113 different cannabinoids identified. Only in the 1990s did scientists first discover endocannabinoids and the body's endocannabinoid system. Endocannabinoids are natural cannabis-like molecules produced by the human body. Scientists began to realize that cannabis affects the human body by mimicking our endocannabinoids. It's thought that the main function of the endocannabinoid system is to maintain bodily equilibrium in response to outside changes that can impact the body's systems. Endocannabinoids regulate the body. The endo-cannabinoid system is believed to exist in all vertebrates including mammals, reptiles, birds, fish, and amphibians. They all produce endocannabinoids.

Initially, researchers suggested that endocannabinoid receptors were only present in the brain and nerve system. Scientists later found that the endocannabinoid system is present throughout the body including skin, blood vessels, immune system, muscle, bone, and all the major organs. The endocannabinoid receptors are involved in a wide variety of bodily processes including pain, memory, mood, metabolism, appetite, sleep, and even the reproductive system.

The Cannabis Market Is Growing

Projections vary, but numbers from Arcview Market Research and BDS Analytics put the 2018 total global market for legal sales at $10.9 billion. Estimated 2019 global cannabis sales jumped to $14.9 billion. According to their report, total worldwide legal sales should exceed $40 billion by 2024.

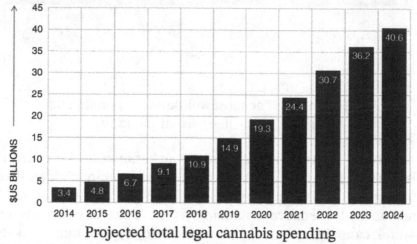

Projected total legal cannabis spending
Source: Intro-Blue, Arcview Market Research, and BDS Analytics.

Among all cannabis transactions, the United States is by far the market leader. Using information from New Frontier Data, total legal cannabis spending in regulated US dispensaries was more than $10 billion in 2018. The US market alone is forecast to grow to $27 billion by 2024.

As regulated cannabis experiences terrific growth, the legal market is still dwarfed by the illicit market. New Frontier claims that US black-market cannabis sales were an estimated $64.3 billion for 2018, more than six times the nationwide legal sales of $10 billion. Of course, in many states there is no legal cannabis business at all. The state of California is the largest legal marijuana market in the world by annual sales. In 2019, it is estimated that California's illegal sales of around $7.5 billion will vastly exceed the legal transactions of only $2.8 billion.

Recreational marijuana sales are legal throughout Canada, but analysts at Scotiabank estimate that the black market would still be responsible for a full 71% of that country's total cannabis sales for 2019.

The marijuana black market will always exist and may outpace the legal market indefinitely, but it also represents a gargantuan opportunity rarely found in any industry. Projections call for a slow progression from illegal marijuana business to legal. Simply put, while a percentage of the population may be comfortable with buying marijuana illicitly, a great many new marijuana and CBD consumers are not. It is thought that the gradual transition from illicit marijuana sales to proper, legal sales could prolong the growth rate of legal cannabis for decades into the future.

Chapter 4
Buy Low, Sell High?

"Buy when there's blood in the streets, even if the blood is your own."
– Baron Rothschild

I've always said that cannabis stocks would be volatile. Volatility doesn't just mean going up or down a great deal each day or each week. Volatility can mean extreme losses for months or years on end. Volatility can mean losses so severe that recovery seems impossible. Volatility and serious losses can shake investor confidence to the core. In the worst of times, many investors chose to cut their losses and search for greener pastures or more stable investments. But as eighteenth-century banker Baron Sir Nathan Rothschild famously said, "Buy when there's blood in the streets, even if the blood is your own." His advice is easier said than done. It takes a very long-term perspective and a firm hand to invest successfully in new and extremely volatile sectors of the market.

Some of the world's most renowned companies and best-performing stocks were also some of the most volatile early in their lives. It seems like a no-brainer to have invested in Amazon or Apple or Netflix in their early years. But these companies weren't always loved. They can serve as great examples of just how volatile and out of favor a stock can be.

Amazon

Like alcohol stocks in the 1930s or cannabis stocks today, Amazon was extremely volatile in its early years. Many people didn't think Amazon would even survive, like many "dot coms" of the era. Does anyone even remember that Amazon began as an internet bookseller? Amazon was founded in 1994. Although it went public in 1997, it didn't have its first profit until 2001. Four years is a long time for a public company to burn capital. Amazon lost several billion dollars in its first few years while building its brand and gaining market share. An investor putting $10,000 into Amazon in June of 1997, would have seen it grow to $689,130 just 22 months later in April of 1999. An extremely nice profit.

Amazon stock dropped more than 79% in 2000 and another 30% in 2001. An investor putting $10,000 into Amazon stock in December of 1999 would have seen it drop to only $560 by October of 2001. A rather staggering loss. Almost no one was thinking of "buying low" at that point. Many thought Amazon was close to collapsing. A story would later come out that Amazon could have gone the way of many dot com era failures if it had not completed a massive foreign investor bond sale just one month before the start of the 2000 stock market crash. Amazon stock was terrible through the year 2001, but they had the cash to survive. The stock recovered 74% in 2002.

Amazon historical annual stock price data

Year	Year open	Year close	Percent change
2002	$10.9600	$18.8900	74.58
2001	$13.8800	$10.8200	**−30.46**
2000	$89.3800	$15.5600	**−79.56**
1999	$59.1500	$76.1300	42.17
1998	$4.9583	$53.5500	966.56

Source: AdvisorShares, based on data from macrotrends.net.

Over time, Amazon stock has obviously grown into one of the world's largest corporations and best performing stocks.

Apple

Apple stock does not go up every year. It only seems like it does. That wasn't always the case. Like Amazon, Apple almost failed. And more than once. Apple was founded in April 1976 by Steve Jobs and Steve Wozniak. It was incorporated in January 1977. Apple didn't go public as a listed stock until December 12, 1980, but was already one of the world's largest "microcomputer" (what they called them at the time) manufacturers when it did. On that date in 1980, Apple's IPO (initial public offering) was the stock market's largest since Ford Motor Company back in 1956. Hundreds of millionaires were created in one day.

But things weren't always sanguine at Apple. In a 1985 power struggle, Steve Jobs was forced out of the company that he founded. Apple survived through ups and downs for a few years before its business turned ugly. A rather seminal moment came in 1997 following a mid-1990s period of Apple's operating system getting old and outdated, losing market share to low-priced Macintosh clone computer knockoffs, and Apple performing at a competitive disadvantage to Microsoft's wildly successful Windows 95 operating system. Apple Corporation lost $56 million in one financial quarter, 3000 employees were laid off, and the CEO stepped down. In the meantime, Steve Jobs had founded another computer company, NeXT, which Apple acquired in February 1997. It paved the way for Jobs' return to the helm of Apple. It has been said that Apple was less than 90 days from bankruptcy when Steve Jobs took back over as interim CEO in that critical year of 1997.

Apple historical annual stock price data, adjusted for splits

Year	Year open	Year close	Percent change
1997	$0.7500	$0.4689	−37.09
1996	$1.1475	$0.7454	−34.51
1995	$1.3707	$1.1382	−18.29
1994	$1.0668	$1.3929	33.34
1993	$2.0804	$1.0446	−51.05
1992	$2.1250	$2.1339	5.97

Source: AdvisorShares, based on data from macrotrends.net.

From Apple's lowest of lows in 1997, no one thought it would become the global powerhouse that it is today. No one was thinking it was a no-brainer to buy low in 1996 or 1997. In Apple's full history of 39 years as a public stock from 1981 through 2019, 14 of those years were losers. With the stock market crash in 2000, Apple stock lost over 71%. In 2002 it lost 34%. In 2008, Apple lost a fat 56%. The great Apple has been terribly out of favor time and again through its lifetime.

Netflix

While Netflix has been a remarkable success story in recent years, its stock was considered a laggard throughout much of its early history. The story of Netflix's success, and near failure, can't be told without discussing Blockbuster Video simultaneously. Blockbuster was the undisputed leader of the video rental world. Since its founding in 1985, Blockbuster had grown to more than 2800 stores around the world by 1992 and was then purchased by Viacom for $8.4 billion in 1994. Netflix was launched in 1997 and was growing – but competed with Blockbuster in a David versus Goliath sort of way. In the year 2000, Netflix's founder and CEO sat down with Blockbuster executives with a pitch to be acquired for $50 million. The story goes that Blockbuster's CEO actually laughed. Blockbuster didn't think of the tiny Netflix as a threat. Blockbuster realized much too late that an online platform was the direction to go for the future.

Netflix had no choice but to compete. They stayed afloat burning through capital on a tight budget and by doing painful layoffs. They eventually figured out overnight delivery of DVDs and, later, prepared to be an early adopter of streaming video.

Netflix went public in May 2002 at $15.00 per share and its stock was an early success, trading above $70 per share by February 2004. Unfortunately, Netflix stock languished from there. From its early 2004 high, Netflix traded at lower prices for more than four years. Four years! That's a long time to wait for a stock recovery. The stock finally surpassed its 2004 price and stayed there in 2009. In 2010, Netflix stock gained more than 218%.

Netflix historical annual stock price data, adjusted for splits

Year	Open	High	Low	Close	Percent change
2010	$7.6400	$29.4143	$7.0186	$25.1000	218.93
2009	$4.2671	$8.7329	**$4.2200**	$7.8700	84.31
2008	$3.7643	$5.8143	**$2.5629**	$4.2700	12.28
2007	$3.8014	$4.1000	**$2.2957**	$3.8029	2.94
2006	$3.7214	$4.5257	**$2.6529**	$3.6943	−4.43
2005	$1.7029	$4.2957	**$1.2900**	$3.8657	119.47
2004	$3.9164	**$5.5471**	$1.3471	$1.7614	−54.91

Source: AdvisorShares, based on data from macrotrends.net.

While Netflix stock sputtered through the mid-2000s, there were growing subscribers. By 2004, their bigger competitor, the brick-and-mortar Blockbuster Video finally launched their own online DVD rental platform much like that of Netflix. In 2006 subscribers for Blockbuster had grown to more than 2 million individuals, but Netflix had 6.3 million. In 2007, following a leadership change, Blockbuster foolishly deemphasized their online presence in favor of fee increases at their rental stores. By 2010 Blockbuster was filing for bankruptcy after incurring more than $1 billion in losses for the year. In 2020, Netflix is worth more than $160 billion in total market capitalization.

After growing past its 2004 to 2009 suffering, Netflix – like any stock – still wasn't a sure thing. In 2011 after an ill-advised price increase, the company lost almost 800,000 subscribers in just the three-month period from July through September. Investors panicked and Netflix lost 75% of its value by November of that year. It can happen to the best of them. At the time, many investors must have thought that the previously hot Netflix had peaked and may never recover. Of course, it did recover but didn't see its stock price hit 2011 levels again until the end of 2013. Its stock has been a superstar since.

Cannabis

This book isn't about Amazon or Apple or Netflix. Those truly great companies have earned their place in the investing world, and I don't mean to compare any cannabis-oriented companies to Amazon, Apple, or Netflix and the unique successes they have enjoyed. Cannabis investing is just in its infancy. But cannabis investing has been extremely volatile – just like Amazon, Apple, and Netflix once were.

Through 2019 and into 2020, cannabis stocks as a group have been down dramatically. But investors are terribly short-sighted and have very bad memories. Many successful companies, or industries, or sectors endured multi-year periods of severe negativity before they flourished.

Looking at the North American Marijuana Index, incepted in early 2017, cannabis stocks as a group surged in price with anticipation of legal recreational sales in Canada. Much like alcohol stocks had skyrocketed almost a century ago in anticipation of Prohibition coming to an end, the index for cannabis stocks more than doubled – gaining over 105% – for just the six-month period of July 1 through December 31, 2017. (Index constituents are detailed in Appendix III.)

North American Marijuana Index
Source: AdvisorShares, based on data from https://
marijuanaindex.com

Cannabis stocks had plenty of wild ups and downs through 2018, mostly before any Canadian recreational cannabis was even sold. Overall excitement continued to grow with plenty of cannabis companies becoming publicly traded for the first time and later "uplisting" from a smaller stock exchange to a well-known major stock exchange.

Stock prices moved up 60% again to start 2019 before peaking in March. After many cannabis-related stocks hit new highs in March or April in 2019, cannabis stocks as a group began a long downward trend. From their highs, many lost 60%, 70%, 80%, or more. Hype was destroyed. According to the North American Marijuana Index, the total return for 2019 was about negative 31.5%, but the results were much, much worse for many investors who only received the negative performance of the latter part of the year. In another development of 2019, multiple exchange-traded funds (ETFs) were launched mid year on exchanges like the NYSE or Nasdaq, giving investors even more access to cannabis investments. Unfortunately, these new funds were not in existence for the cannabis gains in the Spring of 2019. Most investors in the ETFs only witnessed the negative part of 2019's cannabis stock performance.

North American Marijuana Index
Source: AdvisorShares, based on data from https://
marijuanaindex.com

While cannabis stock investors have been on a very volatile ride, what is the total return for the North American Marijuana Index from July 1, 2017, through December 31, 2019? It's practically zero.

After a sustained downturn, index values at the end of 2019 were right back where they were in the summer of 2017. Regrettably, few people were actually cannabis invested back in 2017.

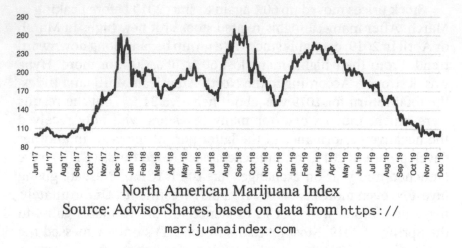

North American Marijuana Index
Source: AdvisorShares, based on data from `https://`
`marijuanaindex.com`

2019

Cannabis faced a perfect storm of adversity in 2019. The year began with an overexuberance for newly listed and available marijuana stocks, only to be followed with the harsh reality of poor business management and poor regulatory execution in Canada, the "vape crisis," attacks from short sellers, an FDA crack down on CBD marketing, difficult financing and fund raising, and the failure to pass meaningful cannabis reform legislation in the United States.

On October 17, 2018, Canada had become the first major industrialized nation to legalize recreational marijuana use. (Uruguay was first in 2017.) With grand expectations, legal marijuana was supposed to eliminate the illegal pot market, generate millions in tax revenues, and provide massive profits for growers, sellers, and investors. Well before recreational marijuana was actually sold in Canada, tiny new cannabis-related penny stocks had already soared in anticipation of what some called a "green rush." Little consideration was given to the government rollout and licensing, or to actual sales volume and profits (or lack thereof). After a year of adult-use recreational sales in Canada, the results have been sobering. Average retail marijuana prices in Canada remain nearly double those of the illicit market. The black market is cheaper than legal in each province across the country.

The Canadian government's regulatory rollout of legal cannabis, controlled by Health Canada, has simply been a comedy of errors. The overall Canadian marijuana market was severely constrained by Health Canada's inability to review and approve licenses in a timely manner. To make matters worse, individual provincial governments caused their own problems. Ontario and Quebec residents account for about two-thirds of Canada's total population. Despite great demand, the two most populous provinces opened cannabis dispensaries at a pathetically slow pace. Ontario was the worst with its ridiculous lottery system for awarding licenses. By the end of 2019, Ontario's 17.5 million residents had just 24 legal marijuana stores. Most consumers are still buying on the black market. The sales bottleneck caused legal Canadian cultivators to pare production.

Referred to as derivative products, cannabis edibles, vapes, THC and CBD infused beverages, topicals, tinctures, and concentrates are generally higher profit margin merchandise. The regulatory agency Health Canada failed again. These profitable items weren't available at all when adult use marijuana sales kicked off, and then were seriously delayed as Health Canada haggled over the governing rules for regulating the products. Called "Cannabis 2.0," the Canadian derivative product launch got off to a painfully slow start more than a year after the legalization of recreational sales.

Short Sellers

As a group, cannabis stocks have been shorted aggressively. Rather than viewing the long-term potential in owning cannabis stocks, hedge fund and other private stock traders saw opportunity to short sell over hyped cannabis stocks. Short interest in cannabis names increased through 2019 and 2020, meaning sellers were shorting at a large and increasing rate as compared to the cannabis company shares outstanding and available. Basically, all cannabis stocks were attacked – good, profitable ones right along with poorly managed, unprofitable companies. Most short sellers begin with fundamental short ideas. They simply believe that they have financial reasons or indicators that a stock price will go down rather than go up. But once they create a short position in a stock, they usually operate technically for the most part in making their short sell or cover decisions. They will short the stock for as long as they possibly can. In general, short sellers believe they can get out of their short positions (cover) very quickly – leaving someone else holding the bag. Cannabis stocks are mostly small cap (total company size or "capitalization" of under $2 billion) or micro-cap (total capitalization under $300 million) and have a comparatively low float (the number of stock shares actually available for public trading). With small companies and much of their stock shares locked up by employees and other insiders, there's simply not many shares available to trade. That makes the stocks very expensive to borrow for shorting purposes and adds to their volatile nature. Even though cannabis stocks are very expensive to borrow, the short sellers will milk their short positions for every penny of profit they can get.

Short Primer

Short selling allows investors to profit from stocks or other securities when they go down in value, rather than up. In order to perform a short sale, an investor must borrow the stock or security through a brokerage firm from someone who owns it, although that's all handled behind the scenes by the brokerage firm. The investor then sells that stock (sells short) without already owning it and receives cash proceeds in exchange. They have an open short position in the stock. The short seller hopes that the price will fall over time, providing an opportunity to buy the stock back (or "cover") at a lower price. (Sell high. Buy lower.) Any money left over after buying back the stock is profit to the short seller. A stock loan fee, or short interest, is charged to the borrower. The cost varies greatly among stocks. When a company's stock is in great demand for shorting, its cost to borrow can be quite high. When it comes time to close a position, a short seller might have trouble finding enough shares to buy if many other traders are also shorting the stock or if the stock is thinly traded. The risk of loss on a short sale is theoretically unlimited since the price of any asset can climb to infinity.

Vape

Vaping usually refers to vape pens or similar devices designed specifically to vaporize cannabis compounds, distillates, or oils. Vaping news following a rash of severe lung injuries suffered by users over the summer of 2019 hurt cannabis-related stock prices, but not legitimately so. The vaping "crisis" of sicknesses and deaths was caused by illegal, black market products usually sold at a lower price point than legitimate products. Evidence pointed to vape oils contaminated with vitamin E acetate – a ploy used by illegal dealers. In a sensible world, it would actually be good for cannabis stocks. No one wants to stamp out the low priced, black market cannabis-related products more than publicly traded companies with their higher-priced, comparatively safe, and legally marketed products. The stock market is a fickle voting machine and cannabis stocks suffered once again on vape-related unfavorable news.

CBD

In mid to late 2019, the US Food and Drug Administration (FDA) cracked down on what they called illegal marketing of CBD. The agency stated that much of the deluge of new CBD products being sold in stores and online were being marketed illegally, had not been reviewed for safety, and could potentially be harmful to users. Warning letters were issued to at least 15 CBD producers and marketers, and the FDA issued an official Consumer Update with safety concerns about all CBD products. Among other things, the FDA claimed that CBD lacked scientific evidence supporting its safe use in human or animal food products. The FDA is evaluating CBD for foods, topicals, and pet products, and has promised reports to Congress while leaving CBD in a gray area. The market does not like gray areas and the uncertainty weighed on cannabis stocks and CBD-specific companies in particular.

Financial Concerns

Publicly traded stocks listed on a major stock exchange usually have at least 70% of their outstanding shares held by institutional investors. That means mutual funds, exchange traded funds, hedge funds, pensions, endowments, and other large investors. Less than 30% of the shares are held by smaller individual, retail investors. That is not the case with cannabis stocks. Retail investors hold approximately 91% of all cannabis stock shares. Only 9% is institutional. It's primarily due to US federal banking laws. The impact is twofold. Cannabis companies can have a tough time sourcing the working capital they need. And a lack of regular institutional buying weighs negatively on stock prices. A large percentage of capricious individual investors makes for volatile stocks prices. Cannabis companies have too often turned to the issuance of additional outstanding shares of stock ("dilution") to raise working capital for expansion, the financing of acquisitions, or just to pay the bills and stay in business. Stock dilution means that existing shareholders suddenly own a smaller percentage of the company. Dilution isn't automatically a bad thing if a corporation puts the new money to very good use, but in reality it can pummel a company's already depressed stock price.

In 2017 and 2018, a couple of huge transactions caused a buzz in the marijuana world and set an early tone for cannabis stocks. Cannabis names soared. Alcohol conglomerate Constellation

Brands bought a major stake in Canadian cannabis leader Canopy Growth in two separate transactions, and tobacco giant Altria acquired a controlling interest in Canada's Cronos Group. In 2019 it became quite obvious that each paid way, way too much.

2020

In 2020, any expectations we had for the stock market, and cannabis stocks in particular, were suddenly and unexpectedly altered by the worldwide coronavirus pandemic. At a time when I expected to see well-managed, profitable, growing cannabis companies finally begin to separate from others, the COVID-19 pandemic brought down the entire worldwide economy. Once again, cannabis stocks sold off indiscriminately along with the rest of the market.

One of the primary growth catalysts for cannabis expected in 2020 was the roll-out of additional dispensaries in badly under-served Ontario, Canada's most populous province. That anticipated expansion of sales in Ontario got diminished by COVID-19.

With US and Canadian cannabis companies already facing a very challenging banking environment before the spread of coronavirus set in, the slowed worldwide economy further limited the fundraising ability of cannabis companies. Many cannabis companies are in a cash crunch. The result is expected to a faster-than-expected industry shakeout – meaning some companies will make it, some will not. There's going to be consolidation. The United States and Canada already have too many cannabis companies, and especially too many unprofitable and cash-poor cannabis companies.

None of these things fundamentally justify the massive and widespread cannabis sell off we have seen. Cannabis sales to consumers are booming.

Light at the End of the Tunnel

Even with the terrible worldwide toll of coronavirus COVID-19, marijuana and CBD sales spiked both online and with in-store purchases. Dispensaries are open and deemed essential business.

Cannabis sales are acting like historically defensive businesses such as alcohol and tobacco. Throughout Canada and the United States, just like people are drinking more, people are buying more cannabis. The resiliency of cannabis sales goes deeper than just a sales spike of consumers hoarding product. While there are concerns from some economists that the coronavirus of 2020 could cause the USA, Canada, and the rest of the world to dip into a prolonged recession, sales data suggests that CBD and marijuana sales would perform much like alcohol and tobacco have performed for decades upon decades – recession proof.

One area where cannabis may seriously lack resiliency, and sales could be volatile, is among companies and locations where the dispensaries are heavily tied to tourism. But in another result of COVID-19, an increase in cannabis online purchases and deliveries could help accelerate a long-term shift in buying habits away from brick-and-mortar stores.

Canada

From Canada's somewhat dud of a 2018–2019 launch for recreational cannabis, the upside is tremendous. Retail stores in Ontario are expected to increase at a healthy pace of 20 new store licenses per month from the rather pathetic number of only 27 stores total at the end of 2019. Those 27 stores accounted for almost 25% of Canadian nationwide sales. While the delayed launch of Cannabis 2.0 beverages, oils, vapes, and edibles weighed on Canadian stocks in 2019, these high-profit products can now add incremental revenue. Product offerings have increased steadily on provincial websites.

It all leads to improved fundamental performance in 2020 and beyond for Canadian sellers. The demand is there. Sales will increase and profitability will improve.

The United States

Contrary to cannabis stock price performance, 2019 was a great year for legal cannabis sales in the United States. While remaining federally illegal, a majority of individual states have legalized medical or adult-use recreation marijuana – or both. More states are on the way. CBD sales are even more widespread. Sales are booming. According to equity analysts at Stifel GMP Canada, total US cannabis sales rose more than 30% year over year for the fifth consecutive year. They now expect the 2020 total United States legal cannabis sales to be $14 billion, and $18 billion for 2021. Significant sales boosts could come from major states like New York that are considering the move from current medical marijuana sales to full legality of adult use recreational marijuana.

Additional upside should come from the regulatory side. Consumer updates from the FDA should lift the gray-area overhang and provide a more visible roadmap for companies that offer CBD products. Most importantly, experts believe that the huge federal versus state law disconnect overhanging the US cannabis industry will be solved in some form or fashion in the coming year or two. US cannabis companies continue to operate with significant barriers to capital raising and banking while operating under individual state laws but federal illegality. All US company operations must be redundant on a state-by-state basis as marijuana cannot be transported across state lines. Financial transactions are a massive hassle to say the least. With widespread public support for marijuana banking, or decriminalization, or even federal legalization, government bodies have taken notice. As COVID-19 crushes economies at all levels and tax revenues suffer, the need for cannabis' regulatory solutions should only accelerate. States and municipalities need tax revenue. US lawmakers feel pressure to act.

Chapter 5
The Movement Toward Legality

"Marijuana prohibition is just the stupidest law possible... Just legalize it and tax it like we do liquor."

– Morgan Freeman

According to Washington, DC, polling and analytics firm Gallup, only about 34% of adults in the United States supported marijuana legalization in 2001. In 2019, that number was up to 66%. Gallup's first data point on the question comes from 1969, when only 12% of Americans favored marijuana legalization. By 1977, support had increased to 28%. In the past decade, American sentiment has rapidly shifted in favor of legal marijuana after decades of consistent opposition.

Canada's Cannabis Act legalizing nationwide recreational use on October 17, 2018, served only to increase America's appetite for legal marijuana. In the US, Americans have witnessed a state-by-state progression – medical marijuana followed by recreational use marijuana. Historically, certain US states that are viewed as among the most politically liberal and progressive first made a move to approve medical use marijuana. California was the first mover in 1996. Year by year and at an increasing pace, other states followed. After years of witnessing a successful medical marijuana program in their state, voters in Colorado passed breakthrough legislation in 2010 to approve the sale of adult-use recreational marijuana. And the Colorado Department of Revenue realized terrific tax receipts. Of course, other states followed. Public support has snowballed as citizens see the successful implementation of medical marijuana programs and states reap the tax revenue. A state's expansion into recreational marijuana sales is simply a logical next step.

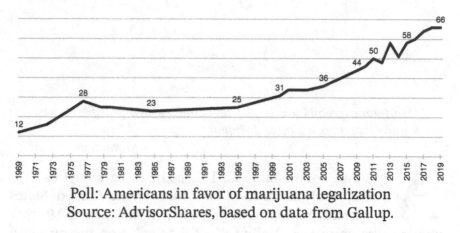

Poll: Americans in favor of marijuana legalization
Source: AdvisorShares, based on data from Gallup.

Gallup is not alone in its findings. In a similar poll, the Pew Research Center found that in 2019 approximately 67% of Americans approved of marijuana legalization. Support more than doubled in the 20 years since 1999.

The Pew poll also asked what type of legalization they support. A majority 59% of respondents claimed they were in favor of both medical and recreational marijuana legislation, while only 32% would want to limit legalization to medical use only. It's incredibly obvious that a majority of Americans disagree with the current US federal policy on marijuana.

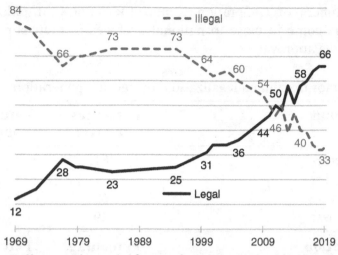

Poll: Americans in favor of marijuana legalization
Source: AdvisorShares, based on data from Pew Research Center.

According to Gallup's research, there's little difference in marijuana support between household income levels, education levels, or by region on the country. Males and females also seem to offer similar levels of approval. All were between 60% and 70% in favor of legalization. However, meaningful differences arise among age groups and political party affiliations.

In general, younger Americans appear much more likely than those in older age groups to support legalized marijuana. The millennial generation, stated by Gallup as born between 1980 and 2000, polled at 80% in support of legalization.

Conversely, fewer than half of those age 65 and over are in favor of marijuana legalization. When looking at the generational groupings, the numbers fall off quickly among adults born in 1945 and prior where only 40% are in support. Separately, sales data supports that a growing number of older Americans are consumers of medical marijuana and CBD, even while not in widespread support of recreational use marijuana.

Members of Generation X and the somewhat older Baby Boomers come in close to national averages in their support for marijuana approval.

Support for marijuana legalization, by age and generation

Age group	Percentage in favor	Percentage opposed
18–29 years	81	18
30–49 years	71	29
50–64 years	62	36
65 and over	49	49
Generation	**Percentage in favor**	**Percentage opposed**
Millennial (born 1980–2000)	80	20
Gen X (born 1965–1979)	63	36
Baby Boomers (born 1946–1964)	61	38
Traditionalists (born before 1946)	40	56

Source: Based on data from Gallup.

It is likely that nationwide support for marijuana legalization can only continue to grow in the years ahead based on the generation gap among those in support of marijuana reform.

Politically, Americans are more divided on the subject of cannabis. Those identifying as liberal or Democrat show the most support nationally for marijuana legalization. Surprisingly, Gallup still claims that a majority of Democrats, Independents and Republicans alike were in favor of legalization, with Republicans coming in just above the halfway mark at 51%. While those claiming to be conservative were slightly opposed to marijuana at 50% negative versus only 48% in favor, it is still rather striking that even the most conservative Ideology could be divided nearly 50 / 50 in their view on marijuana reform. Adding all together, there's widespread support.

Support for marijuana legalization, by political party and ideology

Party	Percentage in favor	Percentage opposed
Democrat	76	23
Independent	68	23
Republican	51	47

Political ideology	Percentage in favor	Percentage opposed
Liberal	82	17
Moderate	72	27
Conservative	48	50

Source: Based on data from Gallup.

The years 2020 and 2021 could be big for marijuana legislation in the United States. The year began with Illinois's first recreational marijuana sales in January of 2020. Illinois is a big state. It's the sixth most populous in the United States, and now the second largest state behind California to legalize recreational marijuana sales. It was also exciting because of how marijuana was legalized in Illinois. It was the first state to approve recreational marijuana sales through the state legislature rather than a ballot initiative. The state lawmakers approved it and the governor signed off on it – both with a great deal of confidence in popular support.

Several states should soon follow Illinois in allowing recreational use. In New York, Governor Andrew Cuomo has pushed hard for recreational use legalization. It is widely expected to pass in the next legislative session or two. Recreational use in a huge state like New York would obviously be a home run for the US cannabis industry. In early 2020 at least 19 states are actively considering cannabis reforms. Eleven states with current medical marijuana programs are considering legalizing for adult recreational use. Eight states without current sales are looking to approve the usual first step of a medical use program.

Adding to cannabis momentum in the United States, the COVID-19 crisis caused marijuana in 2020 to not only be mainstream in most states but now to be declared "essential business" by state and local governments. As economic damage from the pandemic compounds and cities and states face lost tax revenue, cannabis legalization and taxation can only look more and more attractive. At a higher level, the coronavirus pandemic may eventually help with the push toward some form of decriminalization or legalization at the federal level in the United States. As most states or municipalities labeled their cannabis businesses as essential during the shelter in place orders, it further emphasizes the rather ridiculous disconnect between state and federal laws. It only makes sense that a state's essential business should not be considered illegal by federal law.

Unfortunately, the COVID-19 crisis is also a double-edged sword to cannabis legalization. State governments were overwhelmed dealing with the task at hand in fighting the coronavirus outbreak. The state of New York was hit particularly hard. While cannabis legalization may be solidly in the long-term plans for states like New York, COVID-19's impact could cause cannabis legislation to get tabled in the short term.

Federal Cannabis Legislation

Cannabis at the US federal level has been on a rollercoaster through the last two presidential administrations, even while state and public support continues to swell.

Cole Memo

By 2013, with voters in states such as Colorado and Washington approving legal and regulated recreational use cannabis industries in their respective states, regulators at a federal level were pressured to act. Marijuana was obviously still federally illegal. For a state to legalize recreational use for its citizens, it was technically breaking federal law. The government needed to start pursuing strict federal enforcement of existing laws, which would be extremely unpopular, or find some type of palatable compromise. Sitting Democratic President Barrack Obama offered a somewhat cannabis friendly administration – at least as friendly as the United States had seen in the past century. In August of 2013, Obama's Attorney General, James M. Cole, issued what would become known as the "Cole Memo," a memorandum to all US state attorneys general setting expectations for the federal government, state governments, and law enforcement, toward state-approved adult-use recreational marijuana programs. The Cole Memo served as a limited federal "look the other way" policy toward states looking to legalize if those states would implement a strict regulatory framework. It was a big step for the federal government and widely applauded by cannabis proponents.

If a state were to avoid federal interference, the Cole Memo wanted states to:

- Prevent the distribution of marijuana to minors
- Prevent revenue from the sale of marijuana from funding criminal enterprises, gangs, or cartels
- Prevent the movement of marijuana across state lines from a state where it is legal under state law
- Prevent state-legal marijuana activity from being used to cover for trafficking or other illegal activity
- Prevent violence and firearm use associated with the growing or distribution of marijuana
- Prevent drugged driving or worsening of other negative public health consequences associated with marijuana use
- Prevent growing marijuana on public lands
- Prevent marijuana possession or use on federally owned property.

With these guidelines intended to slightly bridge the state versus federal law gap, Obama's administration was otherwise able to avoid questions of federal decriminalization, federal legalization, or even federal banking as it relates to cannabis.

In January 2017, Republican Donald Trump was inaugurated as the 45th president of the United States and at least publicly seemed open-minded on cannabis related issues – rare for a Republican president. Unfortunately for cannabis advocates, Trump chose uber-conservative Alabama Senator Jeff Sessions to be his attorney general. Sessions was a long-term outspoken opponent of cannabis. The Cole Memorandum was rescinded by Attorney General Sessions in January 2018, leaving marijuana in a strange legal limbo. Donald Trump and Jeff Sessions were a personality mismatch and butted heads on a multitude of issues. Sessions resigned following the 2018 midterm elections. While the Obama administration's Cole Memo no longer officially applies, Trump's post-Sessions administration holds an unofficial soft stance toward cannabis. Trump has maintained the status quo by side-stepping the issue at the federal level and allowing individual states to make their own decisions, plus leaving questions of federal reform to the House and Senate.

Farm Bill

In 2018, hemp policy in the United States was drastically transformed by new legislation. The Farm Bill (or officially the Agriculture Improvement Act of 2018) was far-reaching legislation to help farmers. It reauthorized many expenditures from a prior United States farm bill, but also included groundbreaking provisions for hemp. Previously, federal laws did not differentiate hemp from other cannabis plants. Cannabis in all forms was effectively made illegal in 1937 under the Marihuana Tax Act and more formally illegal in 1970 with the Controlled Substances Act. For the first time in the United States, the 2018 Farm Bill gives hemp a definition as cannabis plant that cannot contain more than 0.3% of THC. The bill allows for hemp cultivation quite broadly and allows for the sale, transport, and possession of hemp-derived products, as long as those products were produced in a manner consistent with the law. Hemp can be moved across state lines – unlike the marijuana plant version of the cannabis plant.

The Farm Bill did legalize hemp, but it didn't create a system in which people can grow it as freely as they can grow other items like fruit or vegetables. Hemp will remain a highly regulated crop in the United States whether for personal use or industrial production.

The Farm Bill has no effect on state-legal marijuana programs but served as a huge boon to the development and sale of CBD products in the United States. It was another major step toward cannabis acceptance in the United States with members of the House and Senate showing a willingness to address cannabis related issues.

SAFE Banking Act

In the United States House of Representatives and Senate, a rather constant stream of reform bills are proposed to reconsider cannabis at a federal level. Most have very little chance of ever becoming law. A true breakthrough happened in 2019 when the US House of Representatives passed the SAFE Banking Act. It's far different than hemp's inclusion in the prior year's Farm Bill. The Secure and Fair Enforcement (SAFE) Banking Act became the first standalone marijuana bill to be passed by a House floor vote. SAFE would simply enable banks to offer loans and other banking services to marijuana businesses. The bill passed the House with strong bipartisan support. Almost half of House Republicans joined the near-unanimous support from Democrats. Following the House vote, the bill has faced delays in the conservative Republican controlled Senate. Some version of a SAFE Banking Act still has solid odds for approval. There's wide support for at least some type of cannabis banking solution that will help bridge the divide between state and federal law. There's pressure on congress to get it done.

Other bills that encompass more broad-based decriminalization or legalization such as the STATES Act or MORE Act have little chance of passing in their present form or in the near term. Multiple bills concerning cannabis research legislation and medical marijuana for specific classes of citizens such as veterans, appear to have the most momentum for enactment prior to the next presidential election. Many people expect these research and veteran-related measures to eventually be tied into combined packages that could be acceptable to both the House and Senate for passage.

Significant Federal Bills

Cannabis Banking

SAFE Act (House of Representatives Bill 1595; Senate Bill 1200)

The Secure and Fair Enforcement Act of 2019 would permit banks to service cannabis-related companies in compliance with state laws of their jurisdiction. The proposed Act is designed to open cannabis businesses to commercial banking and would allow cannabis companies to accept credit and debit card transactions. It is aimed at protecting banks from prosecution or enforcement action for working with cannabis-related companies in those states where it is legal. Real estate owners and accountants who work with cannabis-related businesses would have protection as well.

The measure has wide congressional support with 206 co-sponsors in the House of Representatives and 33 (one third of the full Senate) co-sponsors for the Senate version of the bill.

The Senate version of the SAFE Act is in flux as the Senate Banking Chairman asked for additional feedback on restrictions to THC levels, product potency labeling, and the possibility of preventing those under the age of 21 from purchasing cannabis. Elections in 2020 may weigh heavily on senators need to compromise.

Clarifying Law Around Insurance of Marijuana Act (House of Representatives Bill 4074; Senate Bill 2201)

The Clarifying Law Around Insurance of Marijuana Act would protect insurance companies that service cannabis companies that comply with state law. It was introduced in July 2019 and is designed to provide the same protections to insurers that banks get in the SAFE Act. In any final version of the SAFE Act, provisions for insurance companies should be incorporated. I believe the additional bill and inclusion of insurance companies just adds more momentum to the SAFE Act and the continued pressure on Congress to act.

Cannabis Legalization

STATES Act (House of Representatives Bill 2093; Senate Bill 1028)

The Strengthening the Tenth Amendment Through Entrusting States Act would defer to states' rights on the question of cannabis legalization for medical or recreational use. The STATES Act is possibly the best known among cannabis bills along with its high-profile Senate co-sponsors Republican Cory Gardner from the cannabis-heavy state of Colorado and Democrat Elizabeth Warren. Unfortunately, after initial momentum, it has little chance of being enacted in its present form. Congress is much more likely to enact narrower bills that avoid the issue of legalization – or anything that seems too close to legalization.

The STATES Act essentially is legalization at the federal level even though it does not directly address the Controlled Substances Act. Cannabis will still be illegal at a federal level outside of those states that have legalized its use. The currently written STATES Act also does not solve the federal banking problem or credit card transactions for cannabis companies.

With a 2020 election year and control of the Senate in the balance, the STATES Act is a political hot potato with prominent sponsors. It will need amendments but probably cannot advance until after an election cycle.

MORE Act (House of Representatives Bill 3884; Senate Bill 2227)

The Marijuana Opportunity Reinvestment and Expungement Act of 2019 would remove cannabis as a DEA Schedule I drug and expunge many cannabis related criminal convictions. MORE would also add a 5% tax to cannabis sales to create the Opportunity Trust Fund. Its programs would encourage certain low-income individuals in the development of legal cannabis businesses. Like the STATES Act, the

MORE Act has prominent sponsors – although both from the Democratic side of the aisle. House Judiciary Chair Jerry Nadler is the lead House sponsor. Californian Kamala Harris is the key sponsor in the Senate. While the Democratic-controlled House may pass the bill in what would seem to be a major victory for cannabis proponents, the present MORE Act has almost no chance of moving forward in the Senate. Elements of the MORE Act will hopefully survive for use in other proposed legislation that could be acceptable to both Democrat and Republican senators.

Marijuana Freedom and Opportunity Act (House of Representatives Bill 2843; Senate Bill 1552)

The Marijuana Freedom and Opportunity Act would decriminalize cannabis by removing it from the Controlled Substances Act. It also would establish a 10% tax on cannabis revenue and a trust fund for loans to women and economically disadvantaged groups that want to enter the legal cannabis business. Grants would be available to states that expunge criminal records for cannabis possession. Senate Minority Leader Chuck Schumer is the lead sponsor and former Democratic presidential candidates Elizabeth Warren, Bernie Sanders and Kirsten Gillibrand are co-sponsors. While there are many versions of bills that remove cannabis from the Controlled Substances Act, this bill has an impressive group of celebrity Senate sponsors. It is not going anywhere in its present form, but like many cannabis related bills, its wording could soon show up in other proposed legislation. Much hinges on the 2020 election. If the Democrats were to retake control of the US Senate, lead sponsor and minority leader Chuck Schumer would instead become the majority leader.

Cannabis Research

Medical Cannabis Research Act of 2019 (House of Representatives Bill 601)

The Medical Cannabis Research Act of 2019 would establish a new registration process for manufacturers of cannabis for research. With the new process, the Drug Enforcement Administration would annually assess whether there is an adequate supply of research cannabis available and could register additional manufacturers. The bill would also authorize healthcare providers within the Department of Veterans Affairs to provide information to veterans regarding participation in federally approved cannabis trials. The bill's main sponsor is a Republican and ally of President Donald Trump.

Medical Marijuana Research Act of 2019 (House of Representatives Bill 3797)

The Medical Marijuana Research Act of 2019 expands the availability of cannabis for research and would expedite government approval of cannabis studies among researchers. The bill aims to shift the supply of cannabis for research to the people doing the research and away from the government's National Institute on Drug Abuse Drug Supply Program. The bill also addresses issues with the US Attorney General and the Justice Department to allow and approve such research. The bill's key sponsor is Democrat Representative Earl Blumenauer of Oregon. As this bill is obviously closely tied to HR 601, the two bills will probably advance in unison.

Cannabidiol and Marijuana Research Expansion Act (Senate Bill 2032)

The Cannabidiol and Marijuana Research Expansion Act would eliminate barriers to cannabis research at the federal level and streamline the approval process for CBD-related drugs. California Senator Dianne Feinstein is the bill's key sponsor, but there are ten co-sponsors including five Republicans. It has bipartisan Senate support. Like many bills, this one overlaps with House Bills 601 and 3797 but some type of combination of these bills is quite likely for approval.

Cannabis for Military Veterans

Veteran's Equal Access Act (House of Representatives Bill 1647)

The Act could permit Department of Veterans Affairs (VA) doctors to prescribe cannabis for patients in states where medicinal marihuana use is legal. This bill could be the foundation for a final proposal package to expand legal cannabis use by military veterans. Like many cannabis related bills, Oregon's Earl Blumenauer is a lead sponsor.

Veteran's Medical Marijuana Safe Harbor Act (House of Representatives Bill 1151; Senate Bill 445)

Like HR 1647, the Veteran's Medical Marijuana Safe Harbor Act would permit doctors to prescribe cannabis to veterans in states where it is legal. This bill would also offer protections to veterans from federal enforcement for use, possession, or transport of medical marijuana in legal states. Some combination of this bill along with wording in HR 1647 is expected to move forward. Both bills avoid the broader issue of cannabis legalization, as compared to a narrow focus on chronic pain management for veterans making enactment much simpler for congressional leaders.

A long list of additional bills have been proposed or are pending at various levels of federal government. Some are narrow in scope but have excellent odds for eventual passage. Others have little chance to advance but are nevertheless important as each bill adds to the momentum for cannabis reform, and the pressure on Members of Congress. With lobbying efforts, committee action, and negotiation, wording from various pending bills will often get sliced and repackaged as proposals are moved forward or killed.

Other Recent Bills[1]

- A bill to amend the Immigration and Nationality Act to provide an exception from the grounds of inadmissibility for participation in a cannabis business operating in compliance with State law (Senate Bill 3097). The bill would prevent the United States Citizenship and Immigration Services (the former INS) from deeming persons inadmissible to participate in a legal cannabis business under state law.

- *CARERS Act (House Bill 127)*. The bill legalizes medical marijuana that is following state law, establishes a new registration process to facilitate medical marijuana research, and allows health care professionals employed by the Department of Veterans Affairs to prescribe state-legal cannabis.
- *Clean Slate Act of 2019 (House Bill 2348)*. HR 2348 establishes a framework for sealing records related to certain federal criminal offenses including simple possession of a controlled substance or for any nonviolent offense involving marijuana.
- *Combatting Impaired Driving Act of 2019 (House Bill 3890)*. The bill directs the Department of Transportation to provide funding for grants, pilot programs, and other solutions to improve motor vehicle safety and address impaired driving–including marijuana related impaired driving.
- *Department of Veterans Affairs Policy for Medicinal Cannabis Use Act of 2019 (House Bill 2675)*. The bill establishes the Department of Veterans Affairs policy on medical cannabis. Among other items, the policy provides that veterans may not be denied VA benefits due to cannabis use.
- *Ending Federal Marijuana Prohibition Act of 2019 (House Bill 1588)*. Another bill that could remove cannabis as a DEA Schedule I drug, while still permitting states to block its importation.
- *Ensuring Access to Counseling and Training for All Small Businesses Act of 2019 (House Bill 3543)*. The bill prevents Small Business Administration (SBA) service providers from refusing to work with state legal cannabis companies. The bill prohibits a small business development center, women's business center, or Veteran Business Outreach Center from denying services to businesses that would otherwise be eligible.
- *Ensuring Safe Capital Access for All Small Businesses Act of 2019 (House Bill 3540)*. The bill allows cannabis firms to gain access to SBA loan programs, but also removes cannabis from the schedule of controlled substances. It prohibits the Small Business Administration from declining to provide small business loans to an eligible entity solely because it is cannabis related.

- *Expanding Cannabis Research and Information (House Bill 4322; Senate Bill 2400).* This is a wide-reaching bill primarily under the heading of promoting cannabis research. The National Institutes of Health (NIH) and other agencies would be required to create a research agenda to study the efficacy of cannabis in providing therapeutic benefits for certain diseases and conditions, cannabis potencies, risk factors, and effect of cannabis on certain at-risk populations, including children, older individuals, and pregnant or breast-feeding women. As in numerous other proposed bills, marijuana would be rescheduled under the Controlled Substances Act and no longer a Schedule I drug.
- *Fairness in Federal Drug Testing Under State Laws Act (House Bill 1687).* HR 1687 would permit the federal government to employ those who use cannabis in compliance with state laws and prohibits any adverse personnel action against federal employees who use marijuana where legal.
- *Homegrown Act of 2019 (House Bill 3544).* The bill removes marijuana from the list of scheduled substances under the Controlled Substances Act and eliminates criminal penalties for those who manufacture, distribute, or possess marijuana with intent to distribute. The Small Business Administration would also establish a grant program to support licensing and employment for individuals adversely impacted by the war on drugs.
- *Impaired Driving Study Act (House Bill 3888).* Similar to House Bill 3890 but would require the National Highway Traffic Safety Administration to conduct a study on impaired driving to include cannabis use.
- *LUMMA (Legitimate Use of Medicinal Marihuana Act) (House Bill 171).* Moves cannabis from Schedule I to Schedule II of the Controlled Substances Act and allows for medical marijuana in states where legal without interference of federal law.
- *MAPLE Act (House Bill 2703).* Removes various marijuana-related acts from the list of crimes that would permit government to block entry or deport aliens if such acts were lawful in the jurisdiction where they occurred.

- *Marijuana 1-to-3 Act of 2019 (House Bill 4323).* The bill simply directs the Drug Enforcement Administration to transfer marijuana from Schedule I to Schedule III of the Controlled Substances Act.
- *Marijuana Data Collection Act (House Bill 1587).* This bill requires the Department of Health and Human Services, in coordination with the Department of Justice, the Department of Labor, and certain state agencies, to enter into an arrangement with the National Academy of Sciences to study the effects of marijuana legalization in those states that have approved its use.
- *Marijuana in Federally Assisted Housing Parity Act of 2019 (House Bill 2338).* This bill provides that an individual may not be denied occupancy in federally assisted housing due to marijuana use, and the Department of Housing and Urban Development may not prohibit or discourage the use of marijuana in federally assisted housing if in compliance with applicable state law.
- *Marijuana Justice Act (House Bill 1456; Senate Bill 597).* Straightforward – it legalizes cannabis and expunges records of cannabis convictions at the federal level. It removes marijuana entirely from the Controlled Substances Act. The bill would also create a Community Reinvestment Fund.
- *Marijuana Revenue and Regulation Act (House Bill 1120; Senate Bill 420).* The bill removes marijuana from the list of controlled substances and establishes requirements for the taxation and regulation of marijuana products.
- *Next Step Act (House Bill 1893; Senate Bill 697).* The Next Step Act is a broad criminal justice bill that also seeks to de-schedule marijuana from the Controlled Substances Act.
- *REFER Act of 2019 (House Bill 1455).* Prohibits the use of funds made available by Congress to a federal department or agency federal government against any cannabis-related activities that are authorized by state law. Federal government cannot interfere with any state level cannabis legalization.
- *Regulate Marijuana Like Alcohol Act (House Bill 420).* The bill remove cannabis as a DEA scheduled drug, requires federal

licensing to sell or import cannabis, plus assigns cannabis oversight responsibility to the Bureau of Alcohol, Tobacco, Firearms and Explosives (ATF).

- *Removing Marijuana from Deportable Offenses Act (House Bill 4390; Senate Bill 2021).* Offenses involving the use, possession, or distribution of marijuana would be removed from the list of crimes that could make an alien inadmissible into the United States or call for deportation.
- *Respect States' and Citizens' Rights Act of 2019 (House Bill 2012).* Another bill that aims at cannabis in the Controlled Substances Act. This bill exempts cannabis where it is state legal.
- *Responsibly Addressing the Marijuana Policy Gap Act of 2019 (House Bill 1119; Senate Bill 421).* The bill removes numerous federal restrictions on marijuana-related conduct and activities that are legal under state or tribal law.
- *Second Amendment Protection Act (House Bill 2071).* Would allow gun ownership for those who use medical marijuana in states where legal.
- *Second Chance for Students Act (House Bill 4089).* This bill modifies federal student aid eligibility to allow anyone convicted of cannabis possession to retain eligibility to student loan programs.
- *Sensible Enforcement of Cannabis Act of 2019 (House Bill 493).* Prohibits the Department of Justice from prosecuting cannabis related activities in states where it is legal.
- *Small Business Tax Equity Act of 2019 (House Bill 1118; Senate Bill 422).* Businesses that conduct marijuana sales in compliance with state law would be exempt from a provision in the Internal Revenue Code that prohibits business-related tax credits or deductions for expenditures in connection with controlled substances.
- *State Cannabis Commerce Act (Senate Bill 2030).* Could allow legal states to export cannabis to other legal states and prohibit the use of federal funds to prevent a state from implementing certain marijuana-related laws.
- *To direct the Secretary of Veterans Affairs to conduct and support research on the efficacy and safety of medicinal cannabis, and for*

other purposes (House Bill 747). The bill requires the Department of Veterans Affairs to conduct and support research on the efficacy and safety of certain forms of cannabis for veterans enrolled in the Department of Veterans Affairs health care system.

- *To prohibit the Secretary of Veterans Affairs from denying home loans for veterans who legally work in the marijuana industry on the basis of the nature of such work, and for other purposes (House Bill 5477; Senate Bill 3087).* This bill allows those who work within state-legal cannabis businesses to retain access to the Department of Veterans Affairs mortgage program.
- *To require the Secretary of Veterans Affairs to provide training in the use of medical cannabis for all Department of Veterans Affairs primary care providers, and for other purposes (House Bill 2677).* The bill would require the Department of Veterans Affairs to provide its primary care providers with training in the use of medical cannabis.
- *Tribal Marijuana Sovereignty Act of 2019 (House Bill 1416).* Protects production, purchase, and possession of cannabis on tribal lands when properly authorized by appropriate tribal authorities.
- *VA Medicinal Cannabis Research Act of 2019 (House Bill 712; Senate Bill 179).* Requires the Department of Veterans Affairs to conduct tests on use of cannabis for pain and PTSD.
- *VA Survey of Cannabis Use Act (House Bill 2676).* Would require the Department of Veterans Affairs (VA) to provide for a survey of veterans and VA health care providers regarding cannabis use by veterans.
- *Veterans Cannabis Use for Safe Healing Act (House Bill 2191).* The bill prohibits the Department of Veterans Affairs from denying any VA benefits due to a veteran's participation in any state-approved medical marijuana program.

Note

1. Source: congress.gov, 116th Congress (2019–2020).

Chapter 6
Canada Versus the United States

"Canada is not the party. It's the apartment above the party."
                                                    – Craig Ferguson

Canada

Medical use marijuana has been regulated in Canada in various forms since 2001. When Canada became the world's first major economy to legalize recreational marijuana in 2018, it represented a major societal shift and was expected to increase the total market for Canadian LPs (licensed producers) at least tenfold over their previous domestic medical marijuana market. Canada had already been at the forefront of the global cannabis industry by adopting their formal medical marijuana program using licensed commercial growers back in 2013. Canadian LPs became leaders in building pharmaceutical grade production facilities and developing top-level greenhouse cultivation expertise. Canadian producers were positioned to become global leaders of the cannabis sector. With the 2018 recreational legalization, Canadians only needed sales to match their lofty expectations.

The Canadian cannabis industry has glaring pros and cons. In cannabis company valuation, Canadian licensed producers have a big advantage over multi-state operators (MSOs) on the American side of the border. An easy calculation is EV / sales. That is, enterprise value (meaning total company value) as compared to total annual sales revenue. Even while cannabis stock prices have been battered on both sides of the border, Canadian LPs on average carry a value many times that of comparable US firms.

Canada has a federally legal market for both medical and adult-use recreational marijuana while the United States has neither. With the legal status in their home country, some Canadian cannabis firms have been able to list their stocks on the New York Stock Exchange (NYSE) and NASDAQ in the United States. (Just a couple years ago, the thought was unimaginable.) Others can list on the Toronto Stock Exchange (TSX) or the TSX Venture (the TSXV for smaller companies). The NYSE, NASDAQ, TSX, and TSXV are all stock exchanges that won't accept the American MSOs due to their continued US federally illegal status. Canadian firms are legal as long as they keep their business in Canada – and out of the United States. Along with major stock exchange listings come investors. Not only do the listed Canadian firms have more exposure for individual investors, but these exchange-listed Canadian firms have more access to institutional investors like hedge funds, exchange-traded funds (ETFs), and wealthy family offices. Many investors are leery of stocks traded on less-prominent exchanges or in the over-the-counter (OTC) market. Some investors, brokers, and investment advisors aren't even allowed to transact in stocks that aren't listed on an approved major stock exchange. Once a firm can be listed on an exchange like the NYSE, NASDAQ, or Toronto, its stocks can be purchased through virtually any brokerage firm and without previous concerns about cannabis company illegality and associated illegal financial transactions.

With legality, the Canadian LPs have access to banking. Canadian LPs can complete financial transactions without breaking federal laws. Other individuals or businesses can transact with that Canadian LP without breaking federal laws. And banking isn't just about being able to deposit money gained from cannabis transactions. Banking means access to credit card transactions. It means access to business loans and real estate transactions. And legal banking doesn't just mean a full suite of commercial banking services. It also means investment banking. As long as Canadian LPs keep their business on the Canadian side of the border, their business is legal. Canadian broker dealer firms and investment banks have been fully open to underwriting deals for the Canadian cannabis firms.

To go along with legality at a federal level, major exchange listings and banking, the Canadian cannabis companies are available for mergers, acquisitions, and joint venture deals. As mentioned in a previous chapter, the large diversified alcohol company Constellation Brands bought a major stake in Canada's largest cannabis LP Canopy Growth through two separate transactions. Worldwide tobacco giant Altria acquired a controlling interest in the big cannabis company Cronos Group. In each deal, they paid a lot. (They paid too much.) Many think that large, multinational pharmaceutical companies may dip into Canadian cannabis acquisitions as well. They have already been active in Canadian cannabis at a joint venture level. Canadian federal legality means that big pharma can feel comfortable dealing with Canada's cannabis firms for simple things like distribution deals or clinical trials in cannabis-based drug development – something that is still extremely complicated in the United States.

Canadian cannabis firms have used their legal head start to look beyond the Canadian border as well. In another move that is unavailable to US operators, Canadian LPs have signed trade deals and secured licenses to sell marijuana internationally. The international market remains limited in total sales volume, but at least 30 countries including Mexico, Germany, and Italy now have legalized medical marijuana programs operating. The Canada licensed producers had an early mover advantage in a number of new and up-and-coming medical marijuana international markets.

While all of these things have led to early excitement for Canadian producers and a continued overall value advantage over comparable American firms, Canadians have suffered from a severe failure to execute.

Fault lies both with the provincial regulators and the LPs that they regulate. Canada has a rather messy patchwork of provincial regulations where one province may dramatically differ from another in licensure and in the retail rollout of dispensaries. A lack of constancy and severe restrictions on marketing and branding have hurt sales and left Canadian firms' bottom lines to suffer. The mismanaged rollout of the retail channel in most areas of the country limited cannabis access for much of Canada's population. The large population in Ontario simply lacked enough brick-and-mortar stores. The populous province of Quebec wasn't much better. Other areas of the country suffered from alternating oversupply and undersupply. Canada's mess of provincial laws made it hard to get products to the consumers that wanted the products. In 2020, Canada's adult use recreational channel continues to be burdened by an oversupply of product and an insufficient number of retail outlets for sales to consumers.

Everything cannabis related in Canada should improve. After a year of foolishly selling only traditional, smokable marijuana for recreational use, Canada finally launched what was termed "Cannabis 2.0" as a next wave of legal cannabis product rollout. It should be a significant catalyst for the Canadian industry, although the spread of COVID-19 in 2020 slowed new development and distribution. Cannabis 2.0 includes high-margin products such as oils, vapes, edibles (chocolates / cookies / gummies), and cannabis-infused beverages such as juices and beer. Of course, all of these products were already being sold on the US side of the border in states where legal. Canada wanted to be pragmatic in their cannabis product rollouts. Instead, their disjointed regulatory plan seriously handcuffed their own Canadian licensed producers and their ability to turn a profit. It is hoped that these new products will be game changers for the Canadian cannabis space and profitability for the Canadian firms. Consulting firm Deloitte Canada has estimated that these cannabis 2.0 products could be worth as much a $2.5 billion annually. We'll see.

For as bad as the retail rollout of cannabis store has unfolded in the Canadian provinces of Ontario and Quebec, it also represents a huge opportunity for sales improvement. Ontario has planned to open additional retail cannabis stores at a rate of about 20 outlets per month, starting in April 2020. By the end of 2020, Canada's most populous province could have as many as 250 stores – an increase of tenfold.

With brick-and-mortar store expansion nationwide combined with the launch of cannabis 2.0 products, things are looking up in Canada. Total cannabis sales in Canada topped out around $1.2 or $1.3 billion for 2019. It was a huge disappointment from initial projections at the time of legalization.

The United States

The US cannabis market is the largest in the world. Legal cannabis sales in the United States increased to approximately $13 billion in 2019, up from only $10 billion in 2018. That's a 30% increase year over year. And it is already more than 10 times the size of Canada's cannabis market. These numbers are only based on existing recreational and medical marijuana legal states through 2019. Remember that many states get a zero for legal cannabis sales. Wall Street estimates vary considerably, but it is felt that legalization in all states would create a $50 billion market. One analyst suggested that $100 billion in annual cannabis sales could be possible in the United States by the year 2030.

For everything that the US market has, it lacks Canada's most powerful virtue – federal legalization and everything that comes along with it. Cannabis companies in the United States (the multi-state operators), while representing billions of dollars in sales, cannot list their shares on the New York Stock Exchange, or NASDAQ, or even Canada's TSX or TSXV. The US-based MSOs that are publicly traded have typically listed their stocks on the smaller Canadian Stock Exchange (CSE), and then had their shares also trade in the US over-the-counter (OTC) market. Stocks not listed on the major exchanges are at least less attractive to most investors. In other cases, these stocks are completely impossible to trade – depending on a brokerage firm's or custodian bank's rules. US cannabis companies also won't get investments from big pharma, big tobacco, or major alcohol corporations. Deals similar to that of Constellation Brands and Altria won't happen with American cannabis multi-state operators while the US federal law disconnect remains.

While marijuana remains illegal in the United States at a federal level, serious financing concerns remain for US marijuana companies. Banks and credit unions have avoided providing even basic banking services to cannabis businesses that "touch the plant" as well as companies that service marijuana businesses as their primary function. Banking for cannabis companies in the United States is not a gray area. Banks in the United States are federally chartered and would actually be exposing themselves to severe criminal and financial penalties for transacting with marijuana related businesses. US cannabis firms lack access to commercial banks, but they also lack access to investment banks. Large US investment banks would usually bend over backwards to underwrite deals for public corporations with sales in the billions and growing, but federally illegal cannabis companies are off limits. US cannabis firms in need of working capital have been forced to be creative in their financing, often turning to real estate sale-leasebacks or the issuance of more shares. As one of the few ways a cannabis company can raise cash, in a sale-leaseback a cannabis company sells its valuable real estate in a cash transaction combined with a long-term deal to lease the property back from the buyer. It is a better option than issuing more shares of stock. When a cannabis company in a cash crunch needs to raise capital and issue additional shares of its stock, existing shareholder value gets diluted and the stock price almost always suffers. Financing options for US cannabis companies are quite limited while the federal ban on marijuana remains.

While state-legal US cannabis sales greatly exceed those in Canada, high tax rates in the United States do hinder sales. Even while leading the world in legal sales, California sets the bar for excessive taxes hindering marijuana sales growth. California has an already high state sales tax. Combined with local tax, wholesale tax, and a 15% excise tax, consumers may pay more than 45% extra in their final product sales price. Other overhead expenses, such as laboratory quality testing, are also being added to retail marijuana prices. Black-market marijuana still dominates the California landscape. In California and all states, the legal market can only cut into the illicit market at a slow pace.

Federal law in the United States also means US operators must have completely redundant operations in each legal state where they are licensed. Thus, the term "multi-state operators." Companies are not permitted to bring cannabis and cannabis-derived products across state lines. Marijuana must be grown, sold, and used all within the state boundaries. While on the surface, US companies being forced to exist with separate operations in each state may seem like a big disadvantage, it's not necessarily so. It is a major hassle though. Unlike in Canada where the majority of distribution and retail operations for recreational cannabis sales are monopolized by their provincial liquor boards, there is no state intervention in the supply chain for the US MSOs. In the United States, the supply chain of a company is owned by that company. They create, distribute, and sell their own products. True vertical integration exists in most states. Middlemen are removed. Many state regulators – like those in Florida, Arizona, New York, New Jersey, and Maine – even require licensees to be vertically integrated. Vertical integration translates into higher margin capture for US operators as compared to the Canadian licensed producers. With the ability to vertically integrate, the system in the United States simply positions the multi-state operators for higher profitability on average than Canadian LPs and their cumbersome government-heavy retail system.

Quality of Product

With more than 20 years of legal cannabis growing experience, operators in the United States of America have earned the reputation of creating the best marijuana product in the world. California cannabis is widely regarded as among the highest in quality. Humboldt County, California, in particular is famous for legendary cannabis strains. Cultivators have been developing legal marijuana products since 1996 (and illegal even longer). It's all about high-quality genetics and scientific growth. US multi-state operators have mastered the science of large-scale grow operations, and state-legal cannabis cultivation is highly regulated for quality and safety. Operators in the United States are also world leaders with innovations in oils, topicals, and edible forms of cannabis product. The United States has been doing it for decades. Canada is just getting started with their late to the game cannabis 2.0 rollout.

While operators in the United States may have among the best technology, genetics, growing conditions and product innovation in the world, they remain completely restrained by US federal law. Cannabis from US operators would be in very high demand around the world if not for the regulatory overhang confining cannabis production and sales on a state-by-state basis. While cannabis remains illegal at a US federal level, growers are unable to ship their products to other countries or even other American states that have legalized marihuana product sales. If the restriction on out-of-state shipping – and international shipping – of marijuana products were lifted, the cannabis industry in the United States could simply explode and fully dominate the worldwide cannabis landscape. For now, it remains by far the world's largest cannabis economy even while confined to its individual states' boundaries.

The US cannabis industry has its hurdles, but the fact remains that even the current US market is many times the size of that in Canada. And the US market's publicly traded cannabis stocks seem dramatically undervalued in comparison to their neighbors in the North. With US cannabis operators' banking, fundraising, and state-specific operating constraints, they have been forced, on average, to operate in a more efficient and profit-focused manner.

The single state of California is a larger cannabis market than the entirety of Canada. Even the smaller state of Colorado sells more cannabis annually than Canada. And Colorado, like California, has been growing and selling marijuana a lot longer than Canada has. There are currently at least 33 states with some form of legal access to cannabis. Eleven of those states have a combined recreational use and medical marijuana program. The other 22 states allow medical marijuana only, although many are considering the expansion into adult-use recreational sales. Many additional states have legalized the use of CBD products only – so far.

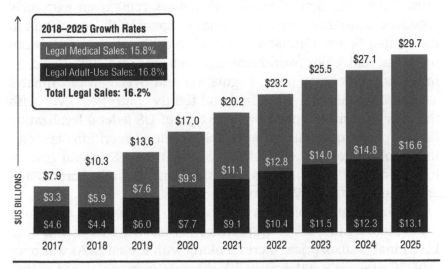

Projected growth of US recreational and medical marijuana sales Note: Sales projections are based solely on existing state markets that have passed medical or adult-use legalization initiatives as of July 2019. No assumptions are made for additional states that may pass legalization measures before 2025.
Source: AdvisorShares, based on data from New Frontier Data.

Canada Versus US Legalization

Of supreme importance to the largest existing publicly traded Canadian licensed producers is their status compared to pending legislative changes in the United States. A number of people that follow the cannabis investment space and track the largest

Canadian stocks listed on major US exchanges seem to get excited with the prospects for additional legalizations in the United States. It is very misplaced optimism, in my opinion. Canadian LPs are going to remain Canadian LPs. I expect no overlap and no further cross-border transactions between Canadian LPs and American domiciled operators for an indefinitely long future. While momentum for cannabis reform in the United States remains high, one must remember that cannabis will always remain an extremely regulated substance – no matter what happens with legalization in the United States. Cannabis won't be sold like alcohol or tobacco products that enjoy worldwide markets and are dominated by multinational corporations. Regulation and oversight of cannabis sales will remain more localized and tightly controlled. Even with the most optimistic hopes for some type of US federal legalization (as compared to various weaker levels of federal decriminalization), there's absolutely no reason to believe that the US federal government would allow Canadian cannabis firms to cross borders and enter the US market. Why would they?

With legal cannabis sales continuing to increase and additional states set to legalize in the near future, it is only a matter of time until US cannabis stock prices increase along with the sales. As was once said, "Canada is not the party. It's the apartment above the party." The United States is the party. The United States is where the real investment opportunity lies.

Chapter 7
The State of the States

"The United States is a nation of laws: badly written and randomly enforced."

– Frank Zappa

Recreational marijuana use is legal in 11 states and the District of Columbia. Medical marijuana is legal in 33 states. Other states allow for CBD sales only or have at least decriminalized marijuana possession. Only a handful states remain where marijuana and CBD are criminal in all forms – and those holdout states seem to be decreasing in number with legislation each year.

Investment research from Morningstar believes that the United States offers "the highest potential and fastest growth of any market." Morningstar added:

As of 2018, U.S. recreational and medicinal cannabis have penetrated just 8% and 21% of their estimated markets, respectively. Based on our state-by-state analysis, we forecast nearly 25% average annual growth for the U.S. recreational market and nearly 15% for the medical market through 2030.[1]

Many analysts project even faster growth.

The US cannabis market only improved in 2019 with Colorado setting record sales for recreational marijuana, and medical marijuana states like Arizona and Florida easily exceeding expectations. California remains the world's largest cannabis market and continues to expand its sales, even with somewhat underwhelming total sales versus sky-high expectations. At the beginning of 2020, the large state of Illinois successfully came online with adult-use recreational sales and posted terrific results.

States of Note with Current Recreational Cannabis Sales

Colorado

Colorado sold a record amount of $1.75 billion of cannabis in 2019. According to the Department of Revenue's Marijuana Enforcement Division, the $1.75 billion represents a 13% increase from the prior year.[2] The new record amount of sales raised over $300 million in tax revenue for the state.

Colorado is one of the most mature cannabis markets in the United States. Medical use marijuana was legalized back in the year 2000, and adult-use recreational marijuana was legalized in 2012. Originally, the state sought to control the industry and keep it localized by not allowing outside investors. Just in the past year, Colorado has opened its cannabis industry to outside investment and witnessed a wave of consolidation in which larger, healthier marijuana companies have acquired smaller local growers and retailers. It has been good for the state's marijuana business.

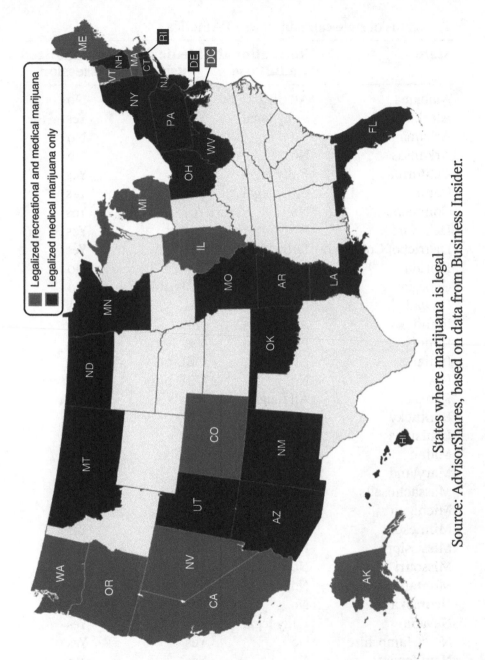

States where marijuana is legal

Source: AdvisorShares, based on data from Business Insider.

The status of state cannabis laws in America

State	Recreational adult use	Medical use	Decriminalized possession
Alabama	All illegal	No	No
Alaska	Fully legal	Yes	Yes
Arizona	No	Yes	No
Arkansas	No	Yes	No
California	Fully legal	Yes	Yes
Colorado	Fully legal	Yes	Yes
Connecticut	No	Yes	Yes
Delaware	No	Yes	Yes
District of Columbia	Fully legal	Yes	Yes
Florida	No	Yes	No
Georgia	No	CBD only	No
Hawaii	No	Yes	Yes
Idaho	All illegal	No	No
Illinois	Fully legal	Yes	Yes
Indiana	No	CBD only	No
Iowa	No	CBD only	No
Kansas	All illegal	No	No
Kentucky	No	CBD only	No
Louisiana	No	Yes	No
Maine	Fully legal	Yes	Yes
Maryland	No	Yes	Yes
Massachusetts	Fully legal	Yes	Yes
Michigan	Fully legal	Yes	Yes
Minnesota	No	Yes	Yes
Mississippi	No	No	Yes
Missouri	No	Yes	Yes
Montana	No	Yes	No
Nebraska	No	No	Yes
Nevada	Fully legal	Yes	Yes
New Hampshire	No	Yes	Yes
New Jersey	No	Yes	No

State	Recreational adult use	Medical use	Decriminalized possession
New Mexico	No	Yes	Yes
New York	No	Yes	Yes
North Carolina	No	No	Yes
North Dakota	No	Yes	Yes
Ohio	No	Yes	Yes
Oklahoma	No	Yes	No
Oregon	Fully legal	Yes	Yes
Pennsylvania	No	Yes	No
Rhode Island	No	Yes	Yes
South Carolina	All illegal	No	No
South Dakota	All illegal	No	No
Tennessee	All illegal	No	No
Texas	No	CBD only	No
Utah	No	Yes	No
Vermont	Fully legal	Yes	Yes
Virginia	No	CBD only	Pending
Washington	Fully legal	Yes	Yes
West Virginia	No	Yes	No
Wisconsin	All illegal	No	No
Wyoming	All illegal	No	No

Note: Most states that allow medical use marijuana sales also allow medicinal CBD. Most states with CBD for medical use, also allow retail sales of CBD based products. Sourced from publicly available information as of April 2020.

Colorado's mature cannabis market reveals the development of interesting trends among cannabis licenses and the products sold. For the three-year period of June 2016 through June 2019, Colorado shows a steady transitional move from medical marijuana products to increasing recreational use. The number of medical marijuana dispensary licenses decreased 14% while recreational adult-use dispensaries increased 30%. It is a pattern expected as other states add recreation use.

Colorado medical business license, change June 2016–June 2019

Dispensary	−14%
Cultivation facility	−19%
Product manufacturer	−3%

Colorado adult-use / recreational business license, change June 2016–June 2019

Dispensary	30%
Cultivation facility	23%
Product manufacturer	49%

Source: Based on information from New Frontier Data.

Over the same three-year time period, recreational adult-use cannabis flower products, cannabis-based oil concentrates, and cannabis edibles all experienced huge increases in total sales.

Change in product sold, June 2016–June 2019

	Medical	Adult-use
Flower (pounds)	−26%	+635%
Concentrate oil (pounds)	+65%	+251%
Edibles (units)	−13%	+357%

Source: Based on information from New Frontier Data.

California

California's cannabis market is an enigma. As already discussed, it's the world's largest cannabis market in total sales. California's cannabis industry has plenty of problems, but also plenty of additional potential. Legal sales of adult-use cannabis in California topped $2.8 billion – far larger than any other state and more than double the entire county of Canada.

At the same time, the illicit market continues to thrive with illegal sales many times that of the legal market. Taxes on legal marijuana sales in California are widely regarded as too high. But each year legal sales are expected to continue to increase and should begin to cut into the overall illicit market – however slowly. More retail outlets are needed in California to create a truly adequate marketplace for all consumers. A majority of cities and counties across the state still haven't allowed cannabis business licensing and continue to oppose recreational use marijuana dispensaries within their borders. As municipalities and counties see successful cannabis programs in neighboring locations – and the tax revenue that follows – licensing should continue to grow.

Analysts at New Frontier Data have stated that California's legal adult-use cannabis sales could reach $3.5 billion for calendar year 2020 and could grow to a projected $5 billion by 2025.[3]

Illinois

Regulators got it right in Illinois. Illinois began recreational adult-use cannabis sales on January 1, 2020 – and Illinois is a big state with about 13 million residents. Cannabis business owners in Illinois claim to be pleased with the overall rollout of the new recreational market. Illinois licensing was well organized across 17 regions of the state based on population. In 2019, with a medical marijuana only program, Illinois serviced about 100,000 patients and sold about $250 million worth of cannabis. Marijuana Business Daily projects that the Illinois recreational-use cannabis program could soon reach up to $2.5 billion a year in sales.[4] The tourist market can be a large driver of sales with Illinois, and Chicago in particular, regularly receiving nearly 100 million tourists per year on average.

So far, demand continues to outweigh supply, as Illinois operators continue to build out new production operations and increase total cannabis supply. More retail stores are scheduled to open each year up to a pre-planned maximum. More product and better access for consumers should lead to steadily increasing sales for years to come.

Illinois regulators were well aware of missteps in Canada's regulatory regime and prior bumps in the road for a few early movers in the United States. Illinois did things right in 2020 and should serve as a perfect model for additional states looking to expand from medical marijuana sales to a full recreational adult-use program.

Michigan

Recreational adult-use cannabis sales began in Michigan on December 1, 2019. Unfortunately, many of Michigan's municipalities have remained opposed to recreational marijuana business. When the recreational-use rules were created in Michigan, regulators put no limits on the number of recreational marijuana businesses that could be opened. They gave municipalities the choice of whether to opt in or not. In Michigan's first month of sales, almost 80% of the cities and towns in the state had opted out of allowing adult-use cannabis sales.

For the areas that are selling cannabis products, demand is outpacing the supply. Recreational growers are ramping up production and bringing new cultivation facilities online. It is also said that Michigan's strict testing standards have caused a bottleneck in the supply chain, adding further to their marijuana shortage. Strict quality standards and strong product demand are both good things in the long run and should lead to profitable pricing. The supply should be worked out with time.

With steadily increasing production, Marijuana Business Daily estimates that Michigan's annual recreational marijuana sales could reach $1.4 billion to $1.7 billion per year when the market reaches maturity. Michigan's existing medical marijuana program already sells in the ballpark of $1 billion of cannabis per year.[5] Michigan is a big state with a very large population of legal age, young adults and potential recreational cannabis customers.

Nevada

Nevada started legal recreational cannabis sales in 2017. The overall cannabis market in Nevada continues to grow at a healthy rate – despite plenty of hassles with its licensing program. Las Vegas's Clark County and its average of 45 million tourists a year account for about 80% of Nevada total sales. The Nevada Dispensary Association says that combined medical and recreational cannabis sales amounted to $639 million in fiscal 2019 (ending June 30) compared to $530 million for the prior year.[6] As Las Vegas makes up the bulk of the states' sales, Nevada's cannabis business should be particularly hard hit by COVID-19 in 2020. For those people already in Nevada, cannabis businesses were deemed essential, and marijuana sales to locals still thrived.

Oregon

With all the talk of American states with fantastic cannabis sales, there are states where it was not always so great. Oregon is an established market with legal recreational cannabis since 2015. Regulators originally set a low barrier to entry for cannabis growers in the state and overproduction drove Oregon's cannabis prices to a low point. According to a recent study, Oregon has more marijuana retail stores per capita than any other state.[7] While that should be a positive, it is too many. With limited profit potential, some growers were forced out of business. Other licensed producers scaled back cultivation when the market was too unfavorable. Oregon has also seen some marijuana growers shift to hemp production for opportunities in the CBD market.

With maturity over a few years' time, the marijuana operators that remained are now enjoying a healthier market with steadily increasing demand. The supply is coming more in line with demand and prices have turned more favorable for cannabis operators.

According to Oregon Liquor Control Commission data, cannabis stores in Oregon sold about $793 million in cannabis products to consumers in 2019 – a $150 million increase over the prior year.[8] The 2019 sales generated approximately $110 million in state and county tax revenues. In 2020, Oregon's cannabis sales should increase to nearly $1 billion.

Washington

Washington State's cannabis market is complicated. With sales exceeding $1 billion in 2018 and 2019, Washington's adult-use recreational cannabis market is the third largest in the United States by revenue, behind just California and Colorado. On the other hand, Washington state, like Oregon, has seen a wild ride and challenging market for cannabis operators. Retail sales of recreational marijuana began in 2014, making Washington one of the oldest cannabis markets in the United States, behind only Colorado. Unfortunately, the state issued far too many licenses in its early years, leading to an oversaturated market long ago.

Washington has experienced several years of oversupply and cannabis flower prices have been some of the lowest in the country. With very low marijuana prices, Washington also sports one of the lowest levels in the nation for illicit sales. Low prices are fortunate for consumers because Washington also charges a 37% excise tax – the highest in the nation.

The pricing is hard on cannabis operators in the state. Smaller operators have gone out of business with tough profit margins and stiff competition. Even with all the negatives in Washington State, New Frontier Data estimates cannabis sales in the state could possibly exceed $2 billion in 2020 from increased production and competition that will continue to hold down prices and encourage consumers to buy legally instead of on the black market.[9]

States of Note with Medical Markets Only

Florida

Florida's first medical marijuana dispensary opened back in 2016, although without allowing smokable flower. Florida's medical cannabis industry originally consisted of only derivatives such as cannabis oils and related products. Florida lawmakers repealed the state's ban on smokable medical marijuana sales in March 2019, and Florida's medical market has seen unprecedented growth.

According to estimates from Arcview Market Research and BDS Analytics, Florida's 2019 medical marijuana program accounted for about $1 billion in total sales.[10] In recent data from the Office of Medical Marijuana Use (OMMU), the state had over 260,000 qualified medical marijuana patients and 2,500 qualified physicians.[11] The patient count is still a tiny percentage of Florida's population of 21 million.

Florida appears to be an excellent candidate for expansion into adult-use recreational sales. A poll from October 2019 by the organization Make it Legal Florida claimed that 67% of likely voters would support cannabis legalization.[12] The Make It Legal Florida ballot initiative did not gain enough required signatures to make it on the 2020 ballot. The group has stated that it will focus on getting recreational marijuana added to the Florida ballot for 2022.

Arizona

Medical marijuana was made legal in Arizona by a statewide ballot measure in 2010. According to data from the Arizona Department of Health Services, Arizona's dispensaries sold 165,722 pounds of medical marijuana in 2019, or more than 35% over the prior year.[13] Estimates from Arcview Market Research and BDS Analytics, put the total Arizona sales at about $705 million.[14] Arizona has one of the nation's highest percentages for medical marijuana patients as compared to the state's population at about 3%.

The Arizona Department of Health Services showed an 18% increase in patients registered to purchase marijuana. The Department has almost 220,000 people in the Arizona medical cannabis program as of 2019.

Arizona's cannabis activists plan to collect enough signatures by summer to get recreational use marijuana legalization on the ballot for November 2020. Legalization is believed to have a good chance of success if it makes the ballot. A similar ballot initiative was only narrowly defeated back in 2016. Public support has only increased since that time.

Potential New Legislation

It is widely believed that as many as 16 states could legalize new adult-use or medical marijuana in 2020 through their legislatures or ballot measures. The COVID-19 outbreak has hindered some states' initiatives, with state legislatures focused on pandemic damage control or signature campaigns cancelled before completion. A handful of new state measures will still likely pass. Much of the focus had been on the East Coast where states like New York, New Jersey, and Connecticut have been in communication on the regional ramifications of cannabis legalization. Cannabis reform in populous states on America's East Coast could create billions of dollars in business opportunities, and many millions of dollars in tax revenues.

In past years, cannabis legalization was usually passed through a ballot initiative and popular vote. In a major 2019 development, Illinois' very confident legislature voted to legalize the state's adult-use program through legislative action and without going to the ballot. The trend should continue in states where the legislature and governor are in agreement and enjoy public support for cannabis legalization.

Other States Pending New Cannabis Reform[15]

Recreational Marijuana by State Legislature

New York

New York Governor Andrew Cuomo has pledged to legalize recreational cannabis in New York and projects that legalizing marijuana will generate $300 million annually in tax revenues. Expecting passage, he confidently included marijuana legalization in his fiscal year 2021 budget proposal. In the New York legislature, the "Marijuana Regulation and Taxation Act" is highly supported but appears to need additional negotiation concerning various social equity aspects before it can be made final. In January 2020, a Siena College poll showed support for legalization in New York at an all-time high of 58% in favor. With COVID-19 hitting New York with more cases than any other state, new legislation may be derailed for 2020 passage.[16] The approval of adult-use recreational marijuana sales in New York seems to only be a matter of when, not if. New York will need the tax revenues.

Connecticut

Connecticut is in a group of neighboring states with New York considering the approval of recreational cannabis sales. In May 2019, Connecticut's Senate Finance Committee approved a bill that could legalize and tax recreational marijuana. The bill needs to advance through the Connecticut legislature, but Democrat Governor Ned Lamont is already on record for his support of marijuana legalization and would likely sign such a bill if it reaches his desk.

Lamont has worked closely with New York's Governor Cuomo in hopes of developing a regional approach for cannabis regulation.

Delaware

In June 2019, Delaware's House Revenue & Finance Committee cleared House Bill 110 that would legalize adult-use recreational marijuana. It is proposed that a 15% tax would be charged at the point of sale. A similar bill failed in the Delaware House in 2018, although Delaware does have a successful medical marijuana program in place already. While the bill seems to have solid public and legislative support, it has yet to gain the 60% needed for the legislature's approval. Proponents want to cut into Delaware's cannabis black market, but Delaware's house members have yet to get in agreement on the full details of regulation.

Pennsylvania

As of early 2020, multiple bills that could legalize recreational use marijuana in Pennsylvania are waiting on action in the legislature.

Pennsylvania lawmakers are also closely monitoring developments in nearby states such as New York and New Jersey, and seem to agree with thoughts of a regional strategy toward cannabis regulation. Democratic Governor Tom Wolf has shown support for legalization. Bills have been introduced in Pennsylvania's House and Senate, but the Senate leader (a Republican) has expressed opposition.

Recreational Marijuana Approval by Ballot Initiative

New Jersey

New Jersey lawmakers approved a resolution that puts recreational marijuana legalization on the ballot for November 3, 2020. It is expected to pass as a 2019 Monmouth University poll shows that 62% of state residents support marijuana legalization. The New Jersey Marijuana Legalization Amendment is broadly written, meaning that with approval, lawmakers would then go back to work on full regulations to oversee the state's recreational marijuana program. New Jersey's approval would go a long way towards a potential domino effect of approval in neighboring states.

South Dakota

In a first for an American state, South Dakota voters will consider both medical marijuana and adult-use recreational cannabis legalization on the same ballot. It's an extremely interesting development for a state where all forms of cannabis were previously illegal. The ballot approvals are solidly in place with the measure to legalize marijuana for adult use officially qualified by January for South Dakota's November 2020 ballot. Sales would be taxed at 15%. South Dakota's Department of Revenue would determine licensing, with a plan to allow enough licenses to drive out black market sales.

In a separate proposal, South Dakota voters will decide on the medical cannabis initiative. In the medical only proposal, local governments would have the power to decide on the number of licenses to issue in their own jurisdictions.

Arkansas

Arkansas is already running a successful medical marijuana program in the state, and two different groups are running campaigns in parallel to gather signatures for recreational use marijuana proposals to be added to the November 2020 ballot. Public support seems solid, although confusion between the two proposals exists. Each proposal differs in numerous details including the licensing of cultivators and retailers.

Missouri

Missouri voters approved a medical cannabis ballot measure back in 2018, and activists hope to get a recreational adult use proposal on the ballot for November 2020. Marijuana sales would be taxed similarly to many other states at 15%. Even with substantial public support, Missouri's signature campaign may be squashed by the 2020 coronavirus pandemic before adequate numbers are gathered to force the ballot measure.

Montana

Ballot initiatives are underway in 2020 to seek a Montana constitutional amendment for recreational marijuana legalization. With the COVID-19 outbreak, a group backing legalization has even sued the state in an attempt to allow electronic signature gathering for the November 2020 ballot initiative.

North Dakota

At the beginning of 2020, a campaign to put recreational marijuana legalization on the 2020 ballot seemed strong in North Dakota in spite of the fact that a similar measure failed in 2018. As is the case in some other states, North Dakota cannabis advocates suspended their signature campaign due to the coronavirus outbreak. I am sure it will be reconsidered for a future election.

Oklahoma

Oklahoma is another state where a proposed ballot initiative was filed to put marijuana legalization on the November 2020 ballot, but COVID-19 seems to have cancelled the campaign to gather required signatures for the proposals to actually hit the November ballot. As an alternative, some state representatives have at least considered legislative action for cannabis reform. Oklahoma voters just approved medical cannabis by a ballot measure in 2018.

Other States with Potential Medical Marijuana Only

Mississippi

Typically a very conservative state, marijuana proponents in Mississippi were successful in getting a medical marijuana legalization measure on the 2020 ballot – officially approved by the Mississippi Secretary of State's office well ahead of time in January 2020. The proposal includes a long list of qualifying conditions in addition to chronic pain. It's said that Mississippi's medical cannabis initiative is particularly business-friendly with no limits on the potential number of licenses.

Idaho

Cannabis in all forms is currently illegal in Idaho, but proponents are attempting to gain enough signatures to put medical marijuana legalization on the ballot for the November 2020 elections. As is the case in a few other states, COVID-19 has damaged the signature drive in Idaho.

Nebraska

Cannabis advocates, including the group Nebraskans for Medical Marijuana, are attempting to gain medical marijuana legalization through a petition drive. The COVID-19 lockdown makes it questionable for 2020 approval. The Nebraska Legislature's Judiciary Committee has also voted for a medical marijuana bill to advance to the full state legislature, but Nebraska's Republican governor has traditionally been opposed to medical marijuana programs.

Kentucky

In Kentucky, medical marijuana approval by legislative action was at the goal line but stopped short. The state House Judiciary Committee had already approved a medical marijuana bill in 2019, but a final hearing before going to the full legislature was canceled with the COVID-19 pandemic. The bill's Republican sponsor claimed that they would have had enough Senate votes for approval but would have to just revisit the issue next year. Governor Andy Beshear, a Democrat, claims support for approval.

Alabama

Traditionally conservative Alabama is somewhat likely to be a state where a medical marijuana program does not need to go to popular vote and can get approved by its legislature in 2020. An Alabama Senate committee approved a bill that would legalize marijuana for diagnosed medical conditions and allow the purchase of cannabis products from licensed dispensaries. The bill would still prohibit smokable flower and vapes. The measure would establish the Alabama Medical Cannabis Commission, which would be responsible for overseeing a patient registry and approving licenses for business that would handle marijuana.

Notes

1. Inton, K. (2020). Initiating coverage of Green Thumb Industries. *Morningstar*, February 7.
2. Ricciari, T. (2020). Colorado marijuana sales hit a record $1.75 billion in 2019. *Denver Post*, February 18.

3. Hudock, C. (2020). California cannabis sales gather momentum. *New Frontier Data*, March 22. https://newfrontierdata.com/cannabis-insights/california-cannabis-sales-gather-momentum/

4. McVey, E. (2019). Illinois marijuana retailers in potential $2B market expect long lines, possible supply shortages as adult-use sales kick off Jan. 1. *Marijuana Business Daily*, December 26. https://mjbizdaily.com/illinois-adult-use-marijuana-retailers-expect-long-lines-possible-shortages/

5. Cowee, M. (2020). Chart: Michigan's early recreational marijuana sales a fraction of their future potential. *Marijuana Business Daily*, March 31. https://mjbizdaily.com/michigans-recreational-marijuana-sales-a-fraction-of-potential/

6. Smith, J. (2019). Nevada marijuana sales rise to $639 million in fiscal 2019. *Marijuana Business Daily*, September 4. https://mjbizdaily.com/nevada-marijuana-sales-rise-to-639-million-in-fiscal-year-2019/

7. Urey, B. (2020). Oregon ranks number one for dispensaries per capita. *The Corvallis Advocate*, January 31. https://www.corvallisadvocate.com/2020/oregon-ranks-number-one-for-dispensaries-per-capita/

8. Roig, S. (2020). Oregon cannabis sales top $790 million last year. *The Bend Bulletin*, January 19. https://www.bendbulletin.com/business/oregon-cannabis-sales-top-790-million-last-year/article_56d006f6-37bd-11ea-95b5-6bf24985e5c0.html

9. Quoted in Lang Jones, J. and Smith, R. (2019). Tight regulations, high taxes may keep Washington State's $1.4b cannabis industry from really blooming. *Seattle Business*, January. https://www.seattlebusinessmag.com/policy/tight-regulations-high-taxes-may-keep-washington-states-14b-cannabis-industry-really-blooming

10. Arcview Market Research and BDS Analytics (2019). *The state of legal marijuana markets* (6th ed.). https://bdsa.com/wp-content/uploads/2019/07/2019_Update_20190409.pdf

11. Edwards, D. (2019). What you need to know about the Florida cannabis market. *Cannabis Investing News*, December 30. https://investingnews.com/daily/cannabis-investing/florida-cannabis-market-potential/

12. Gross, S. (2019). Recreational marijuana group sues over Florida's new petition rules. *Miami Herald*, December 31. https://www.miamiherald

.com/news/politics-government/election/article238870718
.html

13. *Marijuana Business Daily* (2020). Arizona medical cannabis sales increase 36%. *Marijuana Business Daily,* January 29. https://mjbizdaily.com/ arizona-medical-cannabis-sales-increase-36/

14. Williams, S. (2019). The 10 top-selling marijuana states in 2019. *The Motley Fool,* December 15. https://www.fool.com/investing/2019/12/ 15/the-10-top-selling-marijuana-states-in-2019.aspx

15. Sourced in part from Cowen Washington Research Group, Politico, Marijuana Moment.

16. Hogan, B. (2020). Support for legalizing marijuana in New York reaches all-time high. *New York Post,* January 21. https://nypost.com/2020/ 01/21/majority-of-new-yorkers-ever-say-they-want-to- legalize-recreational-marijuana/

Chapter 8
The Worldwide Opportunity

"La cucaracha, la cucaracha, Ya no quieres caminar, Porque no tienes, Porque le falta, Marihuana que fumar."
– Unknown (folk song version attributed to Poncho Villa)

Accrording to the 2019 edition of the United Nations' World Drug Report, cannabis is the most widely used drug in the world with an estimated 188 million people having used it in some form over the previous year. The UN report states that at least 135 countries, representing 92% of the global population, engage in some form of cannabis cultivation. Marijuana consumption varies widely around the globe. North America easily leads the way with more than 40 million cannabis consumers. But worldwide cannabis acceptance – and cannabis consumption – is growing rapidly.

Cannabis legalization for recreational use has remained limited. Canada and Uruguay have recently fully legalized recreational cannabis, and it is said that Mexico is a major country that may not be far behind. In the countries of Georgia and South Africa, cannabis is legal for possession and cultivation but not for sale.

While recreational marijuana use remains illegal in most countries of the world, more than 30 have decriminalized marijuana possession. Rules around personal use or amounts vary. A number of other countries widely communicate that that they do not enforce their long-existing marijuana laws. The Netherlands is quite famous, of course, with the sale of cannabis allowed in Amsterdam's licensed coffee shops. It is rumored that Luxembourg, which has already decriminalized personal marijuana possession and allows for medical use, could become the first European Union (EU) country to legalize recreational adult-use cannabis in the near future.

For many nations around the world, medical uses for cannabis are already considered much more acceptable than recreational use. In Europe, Germany has the biggest market for medical-use cannabis. Italy ranked as the second largest medical cannabis market in Europe in 2018 based on sales. Greece, Switzerland, Croatia, Poland, and others have legalized medical marijuana programs. Most European medical marijuana is imported – representing a huge opportunity for foreign cannabis cultivators.

In South America, the countries of Argentina, Columbia, Chile, and Peru are among recent additions to the list of places that have legalized the use of cannabis for medical purposes.

Australia and New Zealand have strong medical cannabis programs in place and fairly substantial sales. New Zealand has a referendum pending in 2020 to consider the legalization of recreation cannabis in the country. Cannabis in all forms is illegal throughout most of Asia, although Thailand, one of the key countries for growing the cannabis sativa strain, began allowing medical-use cannabis in December 2018.

As cannabis finds increased acceptance in markets around the world in the next few years, additional developed nations should follow suit and ease regulations around the use of cannabis products. Regulatory growth in Europe, South America, or even Asia and Africa, can set total cannabis sales on an even more accelerated growth trajectory. For now, North America still dominates worldwide cannabis consumption. North American cannabis companies still dominate cannabis production and cannabis sales.

Chapter 9
Canadian Licensed Producers

"I've been to Canada, and I've always gotten the impression that I could take the country over in about two days."

– Jon Stewart

If you are tying your fortunes to investing in just the largest, most famous names among Canadian LPs such as Canopy, Aurora, Tilray, and Cronos – good luck. You are going to need it. I believe there are better opportunities among other producers in Canada, as well as among cannabis companies in the United States.

The Canadian market is expected to remain just that – the Canadian market. While we have already said Canada's cannabis sales should continue to improve, Canada's cannabis market will always be no more than one-tenth the size of the US market. Yes, Canada does also have the ability to ship overseas while the US operators do not, but the upside is still limited compared to additional sales prospects in the United States. On the American side of the border, additional states are expected to add cannabis sales at a steady pace each year.

Among Canadian cannabis firms, companies with a solid balance sheet and strong or improving fundamentals are the best places to invest. Improving fundamentals means either profitability, or a clear path for the company to reach profitability in the near future. While it sounds like common sense for investing in any company, it has not been the case for the investing public's view of cannabis stocks – especially Canadians' – over the last few years. Cannabis stocks traded based on hype and hope for the future, rather than balance sheets or profitability. After the initial hype wore off, stock prices came crashing down.

In earlier chapters, I have already discussed many of the reasons for recent poor performance in cannabis stocks, but all those reasons have now led to what some stock analysts are calling a "Survive and Thrive" environment. Companies need a strong balance sheet with cash to survive and they need current or near-term profitability to outlast the competition. Some companies won't make it. The strongest Canadian cannabis companies will endure and be rewarded with increasing sales revenue as the market overcomes all its problems of the past year or two – mostly related to the provincial governments' disjointed rollout of retail cannabis sales.

According to equity analysts at investment bank and brokerage Cowen and Company, the Canadian market has remained over-supplied entering 2020.[1] Canadian LPs as a group had a tough time selling all their product. In comparison, the US market was undersupplied, with strong demand exceeding cannabis supply. On the other hand, Cowen says that a stock value premium still exists for the Canadian firms, and it makes sense. Canadian firms have a full national legal status and the ability to list on major stock exchanges where US firms do not. Their legal and regulatory status can mean easier trading and better liquidity for their stocks. Clear Canadian legal status also paved the way for the major partnerships between Canadian LPs Canopy Growth and Cronos with huge US corporations Constellation Brands and Altria representatively.

Investing

As I describe many of the most important cannabis companies in this and the remaining chapters, I want to stress that this is meant to offer a brief overview and not a deep dive. Stock analysts produce dozens and dozens of pages of granular analysis on individual companies – and updated constantly. My inbox is flooded with cannabis news and analysis on a daily basis. In the cannabis space, more than most industries, the landscape is changing continually. I urge investors to seek good investment advice, perform their own due diligence, study the latest cannabis news, and search for unbiased analyst reviews. And do not believe just one analyst! All analysts have opinions. Some are extremely knowledgeable. Some are biased. Search for consensus and learn which analysts are the most accurate – and most believable. As a portfolio manager, my job is not to write cannabis industry or company analysis. My job is to wade through the company releases and analyst reviews to make the best investment portfolio decisions.

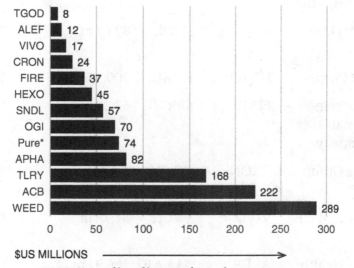

2019 Canadian licensed producer revenue
*Pure refers to the Pure Sunfarms joint venture of Village Farms and Emerald Health Therapeutics.
Source: AdvisorShares, based on data from Company Reports & Cowen and Company, LLC.

Producers by 2019 revenue

Company name	Canadian symbol	US symbol	Market capitalization (US$ on June 30, 2020)	Stock price (US$ on June 30, 2020)
Canopy Growth Corporation	WEED	CGC	6.04 bn	16.16
Aurora Cannabis Inc.	ACB	ACB	1.36 bn	12.35
Tilray Inc.	—	TLRY	962.69 m	7.10
Aphria Inc.	APHA	APHA	1.23 bn	4.29
Village Farms Inc.	—	VFF	277.00 m	4.80
Organigram Holdings Inc.	OGI	OGI	288.15 m	1.58
Sundial Growers Inc.	—	SNDL	87.64 m	0.80
HEXO Corp.	HEXO	HEXO	300.33 m	0.74
The Supreme Cannabis Company	FIRE	SPRWF	67.39 m	0.19
Cronos Group Inc.	CRON	CRON	2.13 bn	6.01
VIVO Cannabis Inc.	VIVO	VVCIF	51.78 m	0.18
Aleafia Health Inc.	ALEF	ALEAF	106.92 m	0.37
The Green Organic Dutchman	TGOD	TGODF	99.27 m	0.27

Source: Publicly disseminated information.

Many of the largest and most significant Canadian cannabis firms have uplisted to the New York Stock Exchange (NYSE) or NASDAQ, while also maintaining listings on their home Toronto Stock Exchange (TSX). Others, like Tilray, listed in the United States without first having a Canadian stock listing.

Canadian cannabis stocks listed on the New York Stock Exchange and NASDAQ (ranked by April 2020 market value)

Name	US trading symbol	Exchange
Canopy Growth Corporation	CGC	NYSE
Cronos Group Inc.	CRON	NASDAQ
Aurora Cannabis Inc.	ACB	NYSE
Aphria Inc.	APHA	NYSE
Tilray Inc.	TLRY	NASDAQ
Organigram Holdings Inc.	OGI	NASDAQ
Neptune Wellness Solutions Inc.	NEPT	NASDAQ
Village Farms International Inc.	VFF	NASDAQ
HEXO Corp.	HEXO	NYSE
Sundial Growers Inc.	SNDL	NASDAQ

A majority of cannabis companies listed on the NYSE or NASDAQ have the same ticker that they use on the Canadian exchange. Canopy Growth's is completely different. Either the ticker "WEED" was not available, or perhaps the New York Stock Exchange was just not a fan of that symbol's use. Other companies such as Sundial Growers and HEXO, like Tilray, are not listed on a Canadian exchange at all.

Canadian cannabis stocks on the Toronto Stock Exchange
(ranked by January 2020 market value)

Name	Canadian trading symbol
Canopy Growth Corporation	WEED
Cronos Group Inc.	CRON
Aurora Cannabis Inc.	ACB
Aphria Inc.	APHA
Organigram Holdings Inc.	OGI
Neptune Wellness Solutions Inc.	NEPT
HEXO Corp.	HEXO
MediPharm Labs Corp.	LABS
The Green Organic Dutchman	TGOD
CannTrust Holdings Inc.	TRST
The Supreme Cannabis Company	FIRE
Aleafia Health Inc.	ALEF
Zenabis Global Inc.	ZENA
Cardiol Therapeutics Inc.	CRDL
Avicanna Inc.	AVCN
VIVO Cannabis Inc.	VIVO
Willow Biosciences Inc.	WLLW
Delta 9 Cannabis Inc.	DN
InMed Pharmaceuticals Inc.	IN

Source: Based on information from TMX.com.

In addition to maintaining the Toronto Stock Exchange (TSX),
the parent TMX Group also owns TSX Venture Exchange (TSXV),
an all-electronic exchange meant for smaller, emerging companies
as compared to the TSX senior equity market.

Canadian cannabis stocks on the TSXV exchange (ranked by January 2020 market value)

Name	Canadian trading symbol
Khiron Life Sciences Corp.	KHRN
Namaste Technologies Inc.	N
Emerald Health Therapeutics, Inc.	EMH
PharmaCielo Ltd.	PCLO
Flowr Corporation, The	FLWR
48North Cannabis Corp.	NRTH
WeedMD Inc.	WMD
Valens GroWorks Corp.	VLNS
Tetra Bio-Pharma Inc.	TBP
Eve & Co. Inc.	EVE
Harvest One Cannabis Inc.	HVT
National Access Cannabis Corp.	META
Sugarbud Craft Growers Corp.	SUGR
Invictus MD Strategies Corp.	GENE
James E. Wagner Cultivation Corp.	JWCA
GTEC Holdings Ltd.	GTEC
INDIVA Ltd.	NDVA
Pure Global Cannabis Inc.	PURE
CO2 GRO Inc.	GROW
Experion Holdings Ltd.	EXP
Eastwest Bioscience Inc.	EAST
Gaia Grow Corp.	GAIA
Geyser Brands Inc.	GYSR
Calyx Ventures Inc.	CYX
CanadaBis Capital Inc.	CANB
Terrace Global Inc.	TRCE

Source: Based on information from TMX.com.

The Canadian Securities Exchange, or CSE, is operated by CNSX Markets Inc. It was first officially recognized as a stock exchange in 2004 and is generally considered a junior exchange to Canada's primary exchange, the TTSX and even the TSX Venture (TSXV).

I do not know that I would consider any of these generally very small, Canadian cannabis companies for investment. While there may be a few great discoveries within this group, most are very small and just publicly exchange listed in the past year or two. Some companies that existed before the legalization of cannabis in Canada have since reinvented themselves with a cannabis focus – often changing names and ticker symbols at the same time. Many of the Canadian companies that are listed on the CSE may trade for only a few pennies per share. If an investor were involved with any of these tiny stocks, I hope it would be done with a great deal of information and solid reasoning. At best, they are highly speculative. One thing is definite – there are too many in existence. Some will go out of business in the next few years. Others might be acquired or merged out of existence in the near future.

Canadian cannabis stocks on the Canadian Securities Exchange (alphabetical order)

Name	Canadian trading symbol	CSE listing date
Adastra Labs Holdings Ltd.	XTRA	01/06/2020
Affinor Growers Inc.	AFI	10/09/2012
AgraFlora Organics International	AGRA	06/19/2014
Alliance Growers Corp.	ACG	06/22/2015
AMP German Cannabis Group Inc.	XCX	09/04/2019
Asia Green Biotechnology Corp.	ASIA	01/24/2019
Beleave Inc.	BE	12/31/2015
Benchmark Botanics Inc.	BBT	11/03/2017
BevCanna Enterprises Inc.	BEV	06/25/2019
Biome Grow Inc.	BIO	06/13/2014

Name	Canadian trading symbol	CSE listing date
Blueberries Medical Corp.	BBM	04/08/2014
Canada House Wellness Group Inc.	CHV	11/09/2016
CanaFarma Hemp Products Corp.	CNFA	03/19/2020
Canna-V-Cell Sciences Inc.	CNVC	08/04/2015
Cannabis Growth Opportunity Corp.	CGOC	01/26/2018
Cannabix Technologies Inc.	BLO	06/24/2014
CannaOne Technologies Inc.	CNNA	11/20/2018
Cannara Biotech Inc.	LOVE	01/14/2019
Canntab Therapeutics Ltd.	PILL	04/21/2011
Captiva Verde Land Corp.	PWR	10/05/2018
CB2 Insights Inc.	CBII	03/06/2019
Choom Holdings Inc.	CHOO	11/22/2017
City View Green Holdings Inc.	CVGR	03/05/2019
CordovaCann Corp.	CDVA	08/08/2018
Eureka 93 Inc.	ERKA	11/26/2018
Eurolife Brands Inc.	EURO	07/03/2018
Eviana Health Corp.	EHC	09/12/2017
EXMceuticals Inc.	EXM	01/31/2019
FinCanna Capital Corp.	CALI	12/29/2017
FSD Pharma Inc.	HUGE	05/29/2018
Future Farm Technologies Inc.	FFT	02/17/2016
Gaia Grow Corp.	GAIA	04/16/2020
Global Health Clinics Ltd.	MJRX	08/16/2013
Green Growth Brands Inc.	GGB	04/19/2018
Hemp for Health Inc.	HFH	11/21/2019
Heritage Cannabis Holdings Corp.	CANN	10/20/2014
High Tide Inc.	HITI	12/17/2018
Icanic Brands Company Inc.	ICAN	04/17/2013
IM Cannabis Corp.	IMCC	11/05/2019
Inner Spirit Holdings Ltd.	ISH	07/30/2018
Isracann Biosciences Inc.	IPOT	07/25/2014
Leviathan Cannabis Group Inc.	EPIC	01/23/2018
Liberty Leaf Holdings Ltd.	LIB	02/10/2015
Lotus Ventures Inc.	J	12/08/2014

Name	Canadian trading symbol	CSE listing date
Matica Enterprises Inc.	MMJ	07/06/2012
MedXtractor Corp.	MXT	10/24/2019
Mota Ventures Corp.	MOTA	03/07/2018
MYM Nutraceuticals Inc.	MYM	09/19/2014
Nextleaf Solutions Ltd.	OILS	09/13/2017
North Bud Farms Inc.	NBUD	09/20/2018
Organic Flower Investments	SOW	01/23/2019
Orion Nutraceuticals Inc.	ORI	10/17/2018
Pasha Brands Ltd.	CRFT	05/30/2019
Pharmadrug Inc.	BUZZ	08/16/2018
Predictmedix Inc.	PMED	12/20/2019
Quinsam Capital Corp.	QCA	12/10/2007
Rapid Dose Therapeutics Corp.	DOSE	12/17/2018
Ravenquest BioMed Inc.	RQB	11/05/2010
Redfund Capital Corp.	LOAN	07/16/2009
Revive Therapeutics Ltd.	RVV	07/23/2019
RMMI Corp.	RMMI	09/20/2018
Rockshield Capital Corp.	RKS	05/02/2014
Rubicon Organics Inc.	ROMJ	10/10/2018
Sire Bioscience Inc.	SIRE	06/02/2014
SpeakEasy Cannabis Club Ltd.	EASY	12/10/2012
Sproutly Canada Inc.	SPR	04/13/2016
StillCanna Inc.	STIL	09/21/2015
Terranueva Corp.	TEQ	12/17/2018
TerrAscend Corp.	TER	05/03/2017
THC Biomed Intl Ltd.	THC	04/29/2015
Trichome Financial Corp.	TFC	12/16/2019
True Leaf Brands Inc.	MJ	02/09/2015
Veritas Pharma Inc.	VRT	08/12/2014
Vinergy Cannabis Capital Inc.	VIN	04/14/2010
Vodis Pharmaceuticals Inc.	VP	07/29/2014
XPhyto Therapeutics Corp.	XPHY	07/31/2019

Source: Based on information from thecse.com. This list can change rapidly and may not be complete or accurate.

The Best

Village Farms International, Inc. (NASDAQ: VFF)

(Founded 1989; headquartered in Delta, Canada)

Village Farms is one of my favorite Canadian cannabis companies. It has a great story. Already a publicly listed company with greenhouse operations throughout North America, they made a big move into cannabis in the spring of 2019. As Village Farms already had great experience growing greenhouse vegetables like tomatoes and peppers, they were perfectly positioned to use their knowledge and facilities in the cannabis business. VFF is the majority owner of British Columbia's cannabis joint venture Pure Sunfarms, one of the world's largest greenhouse cannabis operations. And Pure Sunfarms has been nicely profitable in multiple quarters since opening. The operation is set up to be one of the lowest cost marijuana producers and can price its products attractively. Profitability has been hard to come by in Canada with most competitor LPs reporting notable losses. Village Farms has the profitability that many Canadian cannabis companies are lacking, but they also have a solid amount of cash on their balance sheet. It is not one of the biggest names in cannabis, but many analysts feel that Village Farms' stock price is far undervalued.

Corporate Description

Village Farms is one of the largest and longest-operating vertically integrated greenhouse growers in North America and the only publicly traded greenhouse produce company in Canada. Village Farms produces and distributes fresh, premium-quality produce with consistency 365 days a year to national grocers in the U.S. and Canada from more than nine million square feet of Controlled Environment Agriculture (CEA) greenhouses in British Columbia and Texas, as well as from its partner greenhouses in British Columbia, Ontario and Mexico. Village Farms is now leveraging its 30 years of experience as a vertically integrated grower for the rapidly emerging global cannabis opportunity through its majority

ownership position in British Columbia-based Pure Sunfarms,
one of the single largest cannabis growing operations in the world.
Village Farms also intends to pursue opportunities to become a
vertically integrated leader in the U.S. hemp-derived CBD market,
subject to compliance with all applicable U.S. federal and state laws,
Village Farms has established two joint ventures, Village Fields
Hemp USA, LLC, and Arkansas Valley Green and Gold Hemp
LLC, for multi-state outdoor hemp cultivation and CBD extraction
and plans to pursue controlled environment hemp production at its
Texas greenhouse operations, which total 5.7 million square feet of
production area, subject to legalization of hemp in Texas.

Source: villagefarms.com/investor-relations/shorten

Organigram Holdings Inc. (NASDAQ: OGI; TSX: OGI)

(Founded 2013; headquartered in Moncton, Canada)

Organigram maintains a highly efficient indoor growing facility at its New Brunswick, Canada, location. Instead of maxing out its balance sheet with overly rapid expansion of locations or with costly acquisitions like many of its larger cannabis competitors, Organigram has basically stayed home to focus on growing in a cost-efficient manner at its main facility. They seem well set for long-term success. Organigram has one of the lowest costs of cultivation in the industry without the massive overhead that comes with grow sites spread across the country.

Organigram has also moved quickly and experienced better than expected success with Canada's cannabis 2.0 products. Organigram introduced disposable vape pens, dissolvable powders, and chocolate edibles in February 2020. The new derivative products should provide OGI with a solid revenue boost in future reporting quarters. A recent unprofitable quarter that came in below expectations was disappointing, but at least one analyst referred to it as just a bump in the road, with OGI's long-term prospects looking very good. Like Village Farms, the stock seems quite undervalued.

Corporate Description

Organigram Holdings Inc. NASDAQ (OGI) TSX (OGI), is the parent company of Organigram Inc., a leading Canadian licensed producer (LP) of premium quality cannabis and extract-based products.

Founded in 2013, Organigram first began as a medical cannabis provider. Today, the Company is focused on producing high-quality, indoor-grown cannabis for patients and adult recreational consumers in Canada, as well as developing international business partnerships to extend the Company's global footprint. The Company has one of the lowest cultivation cost per gram among Canadian LPs primarily attributable to high yields and operational efficiencies driven by a relentless culture of continuous improvement and the use of a unique and proprietary software system, OrganiGrow. Organigram has also reported positive adjusted EBITDA (earnings before interest, taxes, depreciation, and amortization) for its fiscal 2019 year and its first quarter fiscal 2020.

Organigram is focused on translating operational excellence into strong financial results and return on investment for shareholders.

Source: www.organigram.ca/about

Aphria Inc. (NYSE: APHA; TSX: APHA)

(Founded 2013; headquartered in Leamington, Canada)

Aphria is simply one of Canada's healthiest cannabis companies. Aphria is larger than Village Farms or Organigram, but remains smaller and nimbler than Canada's largest, most famous cannabis names. It is strong in medical sales, strong in recreational sales, and one of the few Canadian firms operating in all provinces. Most importantly, APHA has put together quarters of positive earnings while their larger competitors seem to continuously lose money.

The company has a nice cash amount on its balance sheet and can keep improving its balance sheet with continued profitability. Cash on the books and profitability are infinitely important in the cannabis industry's current survive and thrive atmosphere. Aphria has that rare combination and no reason to think its growth trajectory won't continue.

Corporate Description

Aphria Inc. was founded in 2013 with a vision to produce high-quality cannabis in the most natural growing conditions. We saw a future in cannabis and decided to apply more than 60 years of commercial agriculture and greenhouse expertise to grow a few medical cannabis plants.

Those initial plants grew into a few million, and we have since become a premier global cannabis company with a presence in 10 countries across five continents. With a focus on sustainability, our state-of-the art greenhouses and cultivation operations, processing and distribution facilities and first-class laboratories make Aphria one of the world's leading fully integrated cannabis companies.

Source: aphriainc.com/about-us

Solid

Canopy Growth Corporation (NYSE: CGC; TSX: WEED)

(Founded 2013; headquartered in Smith Falls, Canada)

Canopy Growth is Canada's biggest cannabis seller both by revenue and by market capitalization. They were the first mover cannabis company to get listed on the New York Stock Exchange. Unlike some cannabis competitor LPs, Canopy has plenty of cash cushion on their balance sheet after Constellation Brands (NYSE: STZ) invested $4.1 billion for a roughly 37% controlling interest in Canopy. They completed the buy over two transactions – the latter in November of 2018. In early 2020, Constellation exercised warrants to increase their ownership additionally. Constellation has lost a ton of money on their investment.

With its market leader status, size, and fat cash cushion, Canopy is not going away. It will survive and grow. In addition to being Canada's largest cannabis seller, it has had significant expansion internationally as well.

After Constellation's second investment in Canopy, they watched things progress for less than a year before removed founding CEO Bruce Linton. Constellation is cracking the whip to tighten budgets and focus on the bottom line. In early 2020, David Klein was installed as CEO. He was formerly Constellation Brands' chief financial officer. Canopy has cut at least 500 jobs, shut down multiple growing facilities, and exited a couple of its international operations. The good news is that Canopy's revenues are expected to continue to grow in spite of the operational cuts. Growing revenue with a lowered expenses profile should lead to better times ahead.

Corporate Description

In April 2014, Canopy Growth became the first cannabis company in North America to be publicly traded. We followed that with being the first to complete a "bought deal," to diversify our platform to include both greenhouse and indoor growing, to acquire a major competitor and to be listed on the Toronto Stock Exchange. Continuing those firsts, we remain the only cannabis company to be a member of a major global stock market index, in this case the S&P/TSX Composite index.

Away from the markets, Tweed, a Canopy Growth subsidiary, was the first to introduce the now standard concept of Compassionate Pricing to make medical cannabis affordable for patients, and we remain proud to continue supporting a patient's right to grow at home by selling the widest variety of seeds in the legal Canadian sector. Our commitment to education has and always will be unwavering, as one of the first Canadian cannabis companies to offer Mainpro-M1 accredited continuing medical education programs to Canadian physicians, and to launch in-person assistance through our Tweed Main Street locations. Tweed was also the first Canadian producer to be approved to export dried cannabis to Germany, and our wholly owned German subsidiary continues to offer an ever-increasing variety of products for sale through German pharmacies. Canopy Growth was the first to strike a strategic relationship with a Fortune 500 beverage alcohol supplier to bring exciting new products to market, and to enter into ground-breaking supply agreements to sell adult-use cannabis to provincial governments across the country. Most recently, in May 2018, it was the first cannabis-producing company to be listed on the New York Stock Exchange.

From our cutting-edge research at Spectrum Therapeutics, to our hemp operations and financing services through Canopy Rivers Corporation, we are proud of our accomplishments.

Source: www.canopygrowth.com/about

Others of Note

Tilray Inc. (NASDAQ: TLRY)

(Founded 2013; headquartered in Nanaimo, Canada)

One of the more globally diverse cannabis corporations, it operates in Argentina, Australia, Chile, Croatia, Cyprus, the Czech Republic, Germany, New Zealand, and the United Kingdom, in addition to Canada.

Even with Canada's problem recreational cannabis rollout Tilray had terrific sales growth in 2019 with revenue of about $167 million compared to only $43 million in 2018. In early 2019, Tilray completed a nice acquisition of hemp food producer Manitoba Harvest. That deal placed Tilray into a leadership position in the hemp / CBD market with products available in thousands of retail locations across 20 countries.

While Tilray has not scored a big purchaser, like Canopy or Cronos got with Constellation Brands and Altria, they arranged a couple of impressive partnerships. Tilray signed a global supply and distribution agreement with big pharmaceutical company Novartis. A deal was originally made to market medical cannabis products only in Canada, before expanding the relationship to the global medical cannabis market. They have also teamed up with the huge beer company Anheuser-Busch InBev to develop cannabis-infused beverages through a joint venture called Fluent.

That's all the good news. Through its various operations, all Tilray seems to do is lose money. In a recent quarter, Tilray posted a loss of $220 million. Remember, 2019 total top line sales were only $167 million. It has posted losses for at least 10 straight fiscal quarters. As of December 31, 2019, Tilray's balance sheet showed $96.8 million in cash and cash equivalents. At the end of 2018, Tilray's balance was $487.3 million – implying they burned through $390.5 million during the year. Tilray's CEO announced in early 2020 that it was laying off 10% of its workforce in an attempt to reduce expenses and be better positioned for profitability. They have a long, long way to go in my opinion.

Corporate Description

Tilray is a global pioneer in the research, cultivation, production and distribution of medical cannabis and cannabinoids. Tilray was the first licensed producer of medical cannabis in the world to have its facility Good Manufacturing Practices (GMP) certified in accordance with European Medicine Agency (EMA) standards.

The company currently serves tens of thousands of patients, physicians, pharmacies, governments, hospitals, and researchers in eight countries spanning four continents through its affiliated entities in Australia and New Zealand (Tilray Australia New Zealand Pty Ltd), Canada (Tilray Canada Ltd), Germany (Tilray Deutschland GmbH), and Portugal (Tilray Portugal Unipessoal Lda).

Source: ir.tilray.com

Aurora Cannabis Inc. (NYSE: ACB; TSX: ACB)

(Founded 2013; headquartered in Edmonton, Canada)

Aurora has been a popular stock. Articles have referenced Aurora as the most widely held stock on the investing app Robinhood – whose prime target is millennial investors. Like Tilray, ACB has built a significant international footprint with operations in at least 25 countries around the globe. Aurora's 15 production sites, if fully built out and operational, were expected to make Aurora one of the world's very largest cannabis growers.

Unfortunately, everything about Aurora seems too big, too fast, and without enough sales revenue to back it up. Aurora's 2019 sales were second only to Canopy among Canadian LPs, but that is nothing compared to Aurora's operational drag. The balance sheet is a mess. Profitability looks far off (or impossible). The company has looked to slash costs with layoffs and other cutbacks at cultivation farms. Following the big transactions that competitors Canopy Growth and Cronos were able to reel in, it was once widely believed that Aurora could do the same. Deals never materialized. Without corporate investor money, Aurora has raised cash through the ongoing issuance of additional shares of common stock. ACB's total outstanding share count has ballooned – and largely destroyed value for existing shareholders.

A stock listed among the most popular stock among millennials on an investing app? Maybe we should consider that as a sell signal.

Corporate Description

Aurora is one of the world's largest and fastest growing cannabis companies with sales and operations in 25 countries across five continents.

Since establishing the Company's first facility in Mountain View County, Alberta, Aurora has demonstrated an unprecedented commitment to executing on its growth strategy.

Today, Aurora and its expanding network of subsidiaries and partnerships provide strategic differentiation through its broad global reach, high-tech, low-cost production facilities, unique product offerings and science driven innovations across the entire cannabis value chain.

A medical company at heart with a patient-first philosophy, Aurora is a leader in the medical cannabis space with a comprehensive program of clinical trials and medical case studies that support the Company's distinct relationship with its patients and the medical community.

Aurora has established early and first-mover advantage in a large number of medical markets, creating strong brand loyalty among a rapidly growing network of prescribing physicians and other medical professionals.

The Company is also a leader in the consumer space, with strong market share, leading brands and investments in multiple retail chains.

Aurora is rapidly developing its assets and capabilities in the emerging CBD-based wellness market. With extensive hemp assets across Canada, Latin America and Europe, combined with an industry-leading product development team and deep brand building capabilities, the Company is well positioned to pursue a leading role in this rapidly developing segment.

Source: investor.auroramj.com/about-aurora/corporate-
profile

Cronos Group Inc. (NASDAQ: CRON; TSX: CRON)

(Founded 2012; headquartered in Smith Falls, Canada)

Cronos was the first true cannabis company to be listed on a major US exchange when it began trading on NASDAQ at the end of February 2018. By market capitalization, it is easily Canada's second largest licensed producer. By sales revenue – not so much. Cronos is thought by some to be on the safer end of cannabis investments since they have plenty of cash on their balance sheet from Altria's (NYSE: MO) large investment, and they should have access to all of Altria's massive sales and marketing resources.

Unlike Constellation Brands' crackdown on Canopy Growth in an attempt to revamp the company toward profitability and protect their investment, Altria has been fairly silent with Cronos. Perhaps everything about Cronos is too silent. At least one analyst has pointed out the firms' passivity as problematic. In at least one good move, Cronos acquired Redwood Holding Group, which gave Cronos control over Lord Jones, a US brand of hemp-derived CBD products. With CBD-only products, Cronos can get some entry to the otherwise off-limits US cannabis market. Lord Jones' sales are light so far.

With Altria's investment, Cronos Group's stock price initially skyrocketed. While cannabis stocks have certainly dropped dramatically since, Cronos still seems expensive. Its low level of sales revenue versus much smaller competitors is alarming. I don't see the upside. I don't see any good reason to invest in CRON compared to other, more attractive competitors.

Corporate Description

> *Cronos Group is an innovative global cannabinoid company. With international production and distribution across five continents. Cronos Group is committed to building disruptive intellectual property by advancing cannabis research, technology and product development. With a passion to responsibly elevate the consumer experience, Cronos Group is building an iconic brand portfolio. Cronos Group's portfolio includes PEACE NATURALS™, a global wellness platform, two adult-use brands, COVE™ and Spinach™, and two hemp-derived CBD brands, Lord Jones™ and PEACE+™.*
>
> *Cronos Group is building a global network, with partnerships, joint ventures, production and distribution across five continents.*
>
> Source: thecronosgroup.com/index.php#about

Considering all of the publicly traded cannabis companies, whether in Canada or the United States, recent stock prices have too often moved in unison – good companies right along with bad. Cannabis stocks as a group tend to overreact to marijuana and CBD regulatory or sales news. The entire group's stock prices make exaggerated moves on a daily basis with buying or selling pressure within the industry. I think it is easy to see a real divergence between the cannabis companies that have cash and profitability, and those that don't. I think we will soon see a true separation in stock performance between the cannabis industry's fundamental winners and losers – rather than stocks trading on hype.

Note

1. Azer, V., Pascarelli, G., Schneiderman, S., Ajzenman, Z. and Vivas, H. (2020). *Cannabis earnings review.* Cowen Equity Research Report, April 24.

Chapter 10
US Multi-state Operators

"We no longer have a free market in the United States, we have a government-controlled free market."

– US Senator Jim Bunning

A lack of federal legalization in the United States makes things tough for US multi-state operators. As I pointed out in previous chapters, the MSOs have yet to be able to list on major US stock exchanges, have less access to institutional investment capital, and don't have access to regular banking services. Cannabis companies in the United States operating legally under any state level law are unable to transport product across state lines. Even when operating in a bordering state, US operators must have fully redundant cultivation and processing facilities in each separate state where they operate.

As a group, US cannabis companies do have something that many Canadian firms lack severely – demand that outweighs supply, continually growing sales revenues, and profitability.

With the lack of US federal legalization and ban on interstate transactions, the American cannabis industry remains highly fragmented and cannabis company revenue more diverse. While a sizable amount of revenue does belong to the largest multi-state operators, many states also license plenty of smaller, independent operators. Those smaller operators, however, do represent a continuing acquisition opportunity for the more well-capitalized, experienced multi-state operators.

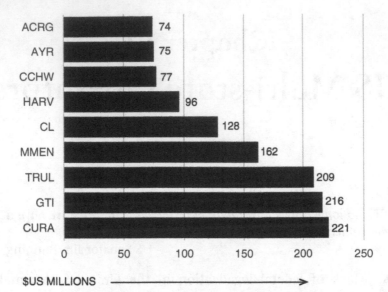

2019 US multi-state operator revenue
Source: AdvisorShares, based on data from Company Reports & Cowen and Company, LLC.

US operators by 2019 revenue

Company name	Canadian symbol	US symbol	Market capitalization (US$, on June 30, 2020)	Stock price (US$, on June 30, 2020)
Curaleaf Holdings, Inc.	CURA	CURLF	2.60 bn	6.06
Green Thumb Industries Inc.	GTII	GTBIF	1.42 bn	9.92
Trulieve Cannabis Corp.	TRUL	TCNNF	1.35 bn	12.60

Company name	Canadian symbol	US symbol	Market capitalization (US$, on June 30, 2020)	Stock price (US$, on June 30, 2020)
MedMen Enterprises Inc.	MMEN	MMNFF	116.60 m	0.23
Cresco Labs Inc.	CL	CRLBF	1.14 bn	4.06
Harvest Health & Recreation Inc.	HARV	HRVSF	108.10 m	0.90
Columbia Care Inc.	CCHW	CCHWF	567.33 m	2.56
Ayr Strategies Inc.	AYR	AYRSF	108.72 m	7.20
Acreage Holdings, Inc.	ACRG	ACRGF	198.68 m	2.56

Source: Publicly disseminated information.

The lists for exchange-listed cannabis companies based in the United States are much simpler than for the Canadian firms. Canadian LPs may be listed on the NYSE, NASDAQ, Toronto's TSX, or TSXV, or the smaller Canadian Securities Exchange (CSE). American multiple-state operators don't have that luxury. If a US-based cannabis company is in the business of "touching the plant," and they aren't a pharmaceutical company licensed by the DEA to do so, the CSE may be their only exchange listing option. With the CSE being the stock exchange of choice for American cannabis firms, MSOs represent some of that exchange's largest corporate clients. US-based MSOs on the CSE range from over $3 billion in market capitalization to tiny companies that trade for pennies.

US-based cannabis stocks on the Canadian Securities Exchange
(alphabetical order)

Name	Canadian trading symbol	CSE listing date
1933 Industries Inc.	TGIF	06/16/2017
4Front Ventures Corp.	FFNT	03/14/2018
Abacus Health Products Inc.	ABCS	01/30/2019
Acreage Holdings, Inc.	ACRG	11/15/2018
Agrios Global Holdings Ltd.	AGRO	11/12/2018
Ascent Industries Corp.	ASNT	08/09/2018
Australis Capital Inc.	AUSA	08/18/2018
Ayr Strategies Inc.	AYR.A	08/19/2019
Bhang Inc.	BHNG	07/11/2019
Body and Mind Inc.	BAMM	12/22/2011
C21 Investments Inc.	CXXI	06/18/2018
Cannabis One Holdings Inc.	CBIS	02/26/2019
CannAmerica Brands Corp.	CANA	10/15/2018
Cansortium Inc.	TIUM	03/21/2019
Captor Capital Corp.	CPTR	10/30/2017
CBD Global Sciences Inc.	CBDN	10/29/2019
Chemesis International Inc.	CSI	07/18/2018
Chemistree Technology Inc.	CHM	09/29/2015
Citation Growth Corp.	CGRO	05/08/2015
CLS Holdings USA, Inc.	CLSH	01/07/2019
Columbia Care Inc.	CCHW	03/31/2020
Core One Labs Inc.	COOL	08/17/2011
Cresco Labs Inc.	CL	12/03/2018
Curaleaf Holdings, Inc.	CURA	10/20/2015
Dixie Brands Inc.	DIXI	11/29/2018
Empower Clinics Inc.	CBDT	04/30/2018
Flower One Holdings Inc.	FONE	10/10/2018
GABY Inc.	GABY	09/05/2018
Global Hemp Group Inc.	GHG	08/19/2010

Name	Canadian trading symbol	CSE listing date
Golden Leaf Holdings Ltd.	GLH	10/14/2015
Green Thumb Industries Inc.	GTII	06/13/2018
GreenStar Biosciences Corp.	GSTR	06/07/2019
Grown Rogue International Inc.	GRIN	11/18/2016
Harborside Inc.	HBOR	03/05/2018
Harvest Health & Recreation Inc.	HARV	11/15/2018
Hollister Biosciences Inc.	HOLL	11/25/2019
iAnthus Capital Holdings Inc.	IAN	09/07/2016
Ignite International Brands, Ltd.	BILZ	09/20/2016
International Cannabrands Inc.	RDKO	09/25/2017
Ionic Brands Corp.	IONC	12/10/2012
Jushi Holdings Inc.	JUSH	12/09/2019
Lexaria Bioscience Corp.	LXX	10/28/2009
Liberty Health Sciences Inc.	LHS	08/29/2014
MedMen Enterprises Inc.	MMEN	05/29/2018
MJardin Group, Inc.	MJAR	11/15/2018
Mojave Jane Brands Inc.	JANE	09/08/2014
MPX International Corp.	MPXI	02/04/2019
MustGrow Biologics Corp.	MGRO	07/10/2019
Nabis Holdings Inc.	NAB	09/03/2014
NanoSphere Health Sciences Inc.	NSHS	12/04/2017
Nass Valley Gateway Ltd.	NVG	03/09/2007
NewLeaf Brands Inc.	NLB	08/18/2014
Next Green Wave Holdings Inc.	NGW	10/10/2018
Nutritional High International Inc.	EAT	03/23/2015
Orchid Ventures Inc.	ORCD	03/18/2019
Phivida Holdings Inc.	VIDA	12/19/2017
Planet 13 Holdings Inc.	PLTH	06/21/2018
Plus Products Inc.	PLUS	10/25/2018
Primo Nutraceuticals Inc.	PRMO	08/31/2018
RISE Life Science Corp.	RLSC	12/01/2017

Name	Canadian trading symbol	CSE listing date
SLANG Worldwide Inc.	SLNG	01/29/2019
SOL Global Investments Corp.	SOL	08/15/2018
Stem Holdings Inc.	STEM	07/16/2018
Sunniva Inc.	SNN	01/10/2018
The Tinley Beverage Company Inc.	TNY	01/28/2016
The Yield Growth Corp.	BOSS	12/13/2018
Tidal Royalty Corp.	RLTY	06/25/2018
TILT Holdings Inc.	TILT	05/10/2018
Top Strike Resources Corp.	VENI	09/24/2018
Transcanna Holdings Inc.	TCAN	01/08/2019
Tree of Knowledge International	TOKI	07/04/2018
Trulieve Cannabis Corp.	TRUL	09/25/2018
Ventura Cannabis and Wellness	VCAN	06/26/2018
Vibe Bioscience Ltd.	VIBE	04/03/2019
Vireo Health International Inc.	VREO	03/20/2019
Weekend Unlimited Industries Inc.	POT	02/10/2014
Wildflower Brands Inc.	SUN	05/26/2004
World Class Extractions Inc.	PUMP	03/21/2019

Source: Based on information from thecse.com. This list can change rapidly and may not be complete or accurate.

The Best

Innovative Industrial Properties, Inc. (NYSE: IIPR)

(Founded 2016; headquartered in San Diego, California)

The first company I want to describe isn't a multi-state operator at all and isn't listed on the CSE. Innovative Industrial Properties is a US-based firm that does business with the major MSOs. IIPR is a real estate investment trust (REIT) that can list on the New York

Stock Exchange since it is a company that doesn't actually grow or sell marijuana. It does not touch the plant.

As I have described already, US companies that cultivate or sell marijuana have a hard time acquiring capital by normal means. IIPR specializes in cannabis-related real estate. Through sale-leaseback arrangements with US multi-state operators, IIPR can provide working capital to cannabis firms in a unique and perfectly legal way, while making a nice revenue stream for itself.

As described by Innovative Industrial Properties:

> *Innovative Industrial Properties acquires freestanding industrial and retail properties from state-licensed medical-use cannabis operators. The properties are then leased back under long-term, absolute net lease agreements. We focus on well-capitalized companies that have successfully gone through the rigorous state licensing process and have been granted a license in the state where the property is located.*
>
> *We act as a source of capital to these state-licensed operators by acquiring and leasing back their real estate. This allows for the opportunity to redeploy the proceeds into core operations, yielding a higher return than they would otherwise get from owning real estate.*
>
> *We work with licensed operators across all product types: cultivation, processing, distribution and retail.*
>
> Source: investors.innovativeindustrialproperties.com

IIPR has a lot to offer compared to an average REIT. Its occupancy rate is sky high since its properties are all pre-arranged with tenants and under long-term deals. It is by far the top player in a unique space, and its market should continue to grow with additional state cannabis legalizations. With IIPR, you are betting on the overall continued growth of the US cannabis industry. IIPR's tenants must have the continued ability to pay their lease terms. Because it's a REIT, Innovative Industrial pays out the majority of its income to its shareholders in regular dividend distributions. Outside of its dividend payments, IIPR's price doesn't behave like an average REIT. Investors know that this REIT's fortunes are tied to continued growth in cannabis.

Corporate Description

Innovative Industrial Properties, Inc. is focused on the acquisition, ownership and management of specialized industrial properties leased to experienced, state-licensed operators for their regulated medical-use cannabis facilities. As of December 31, 2019, 33 states, plus the District of Columbia, have adopted medical-use cannabis programs, and according to a 2019 poll conducted by Quinnipiac University, 93% of those surveyed support adults being able to use medical cannabis, if recommended by a doctor. The ArcView Group projects that sales of state-regulated cannabis in the United States will grow from $12.2 billion in 2019 to $31.0 billion in 2024.

As of April 22, 2020, we owned 55 properties that were 99.1% leased based on square footage to state-licensed medical-use cannabis operators and comprising an aggregate of approximately 4.1 million rentable square feet (including approximately 1.4 million rentable square feet under development or redevelopment) in Arizona, California, Colorado, Florida, Illinois, Maryland, Massachusetts, Michigan, Minnesota, Nevada, New York, North Dakota, Ohio, Pennsylvania and Virginia.

Our senior management team has proven experience in all aspects of the real estate industry, including acquisitions, dispositions, construction, development, management, finance and capital markets. Our executive chairman, Alan D. Gold, is a 35-year veteran of the real estate industry, including co-founding two NYSE-listed REITs: BioMed Realty Trust, Inc. (formerly NYSE: BMR), a real estate company focused on acquiring, developing, owning, leasing and managing laboratory and office space for the life science industry; and Alexandria Real Estate Equities, Inc. (NYSE: ARE), an urban office REIT focused on collaborative science and technology campuses. Mr. Gold served as chairman and chief executive officer of BioMed Realty from its initial public offering in 2004 through its sale to Blackstone in 2016 for $8 billion.

Source: investors.innovativeindustrialproperties.com/
company-profile

Green Thumb Industries Inc. (US OTC: GTBIF; CSE: GTII)

(Founded 2002; headquartered in Chicago, Illinois)

Green Thumb Industries (GTI) operates at least 43 licensed dispensaries with operations in 12 states, plus holds a great deal more unused licenses to open additional stores. Its largest current growth opportunity may exist in the home state of Illinois, where Green Thumb already operates seven dispensaries. Of course, Illinois just opened up recreational sales in January 2020 – and sales are booming.

Green Thumb's primary focus has been on states with supply-constrained cannabis markets like Pennsylvania, where it operates 10 dispensaries and is growing its cultivation capacity. Pennsylvania represents one of the largest medical markets in the United States and demand continues to outweigh supply. Green Thumb is licensed for up to 15 stores in the state. With its controlled focus on certain markets, GTI's profitability profile ranks high compared to most operators.

The company currently holds licenses for up to three dispensaries in California and may soon open its first operation in that state. The California market is huge but highly competitive. With Green Thumb's pragmatic approach to growth, it wants to open slowly in the California market as a test run.

While Green Thumb has had recent quarters of net losses, it is understandable for a fast-growth company in acquisition mode. It has also put together consecutive quarters of profitability in the past. Green Thumb has a solid amount of cash cushion on its balance sheet and has completed sale leasebacks with Innovative Industrial Properties (IIPR) for additional cash. One of my favorite equity analyst firms has called Green Thumb a best-in-class operator and their "Best Idea" for 2020.

Corporate Description

Green Thumb Industries (GTI), a national cannabis consumer packaged goods company and retailer, is dedicated to providing dignified access to cannabis while giving back to the communities in which they serve. Green Thumb manufactures and distributes a portfolio of branded cannabis products including Beboe, Dogwalkers, Dr. Solomon's, incredibles, Rythm and The Feel Collection. The company also owns and operates rapidly growing national retail cannabis stores called Rise™ and Essence.

Headquartered in Chicago, Illinois, Green Thumb has 13 manufacturing facilities, licenses for 96 retail locations and operations across 12 U.S. markets. Established in 2014, Green Thumb employs approximately 1,600 people and serves thousands of patients and customers each year. Green Thumb was named a Best Workplace 2018 by Crain's Chicago Business and MG Retailer magazine in 2018 and 2019.

Source: `investors.gtigrows.com/investors/overview`

Curaleaf Holdings, Inc. (US OTC: CURLF; CSE: CURL)

(Founded 2010; headquartered in Wakefield, Massachusetts)

Curaleaf is the United States' largest multi-state operator, and as I have already stated, US operators have generally enjoyed an easier path to profitability than their Canadian counterparts. Curaleaf has more dispensaries than any other cannabis operator and covers at least 17 states.

Curaleaf has been aggressive with acquisitions. Among other deals, Curaleaf acquired cannabis oil producer Cura Partners in an all-stock deal. Cura owns the popular cannabis oil Select Brand that is sold in more than 900 retailers across the West Coast. Curaleaf announced it would acquire Grassroots (GR Companies, Inc.) in a cash-and-stock deal worth $875 million. Grassroots is the largest privately owned multi-state operator in the United States. This is a big move for Curaleaf for overall size and access to new state markets where it previously had no presence. Curaleaf claimed the deal would make it "the world's largest cannabis company by revenue." With its aggressive expansion model, it has returned quickly growing revenue topping analysts' estimates – but has also had quarterly losses. As compared to some other cannabis firms that seem to have losses with no end in sight, Curaleaf's losses seem reasonable versus the acquisitions it has made. The company seems to have a clear path to gaining profitability soon.

As I mentioned, incredibly important in the current environment for all cannabis producers, Curaleaf has an attractive balance sheet. Even after removing the cash that has been committed for their aggressive acquisition strategy, Curaleaf has plenty of unallocated cash on hand. In my opinion, Curaleaf has one of the strongest balances sheets in the sector.

Corporate Description

> *Curaleaf Holdings, Inc. is the holding company of Curaleaf Inc., a vertically integrated cannabis operator with dispensaries, cultivation sites and processing sites in the United States. PalliaTech, Inc. was founded in 2010 and changed its name to Curaleaf, Inc. in 2018.*
>
> *We're committed to being the industry's leading resource in education and advancement through research and advocacy.*
>
> *Headquartered in Wakefield, Massachusetts, Curaleaf has a presence in 17 states, owns and operates 57 dispensaries, 15 cultivation sites and 24 processing sites with a focus on highly populated, limited license states, including Florida, Massachusetts, New Jersey and New York.*
>
> Source: ir.curaleaf.com/overview

Trulieve Cannabis Corporation (US OTC: TCNNF; CSE: TRUL)

(Founded 1940 [predecessor corporation], TRUL listed 2018; headquartered in Quincy, Florida)

Unlike Curaleaf's rapid expansion model, Trulieve has focused on dominating in their core competency of selling medical marijuana to its home state of Florida. Trulieve's strong business model allows it to maintain approximately 50% of the market share in one of the hottest cannabis markets in the country. It has only planned slow expansion into a few other carefully selected markets. Trulieve plans growth at a pragmatic and profitable rate – compared to some cannabis companies that continually bleed cash. Overall medical sales in Florida are growing at an incredible rate. While controlling its costs, Trulieve has been able to record strong margins and profits.

The company has announced a handful of acquisitions to expand into new markets. A presence in just a few states still puts Trulieve well behind most multi-state operators in the country. Trulieve has a solid amount of cash on its books, plus capital expenditures on new facilities that are already funded. Its primary Florida operations are profitable and self-sustaining. Trulieve has plenty of liquidity to pursue additional acquisition opportunities or continued expansion of existing markets.

Trulieve seems in a perfectly good place already with profits and growth, but if the state of Florida were to approve recreational cannabis sales in the near future, Trulieve would easily be the big winner with its truly dominant position in the state.

Corporate Description

Trulieve is the first and leading medical cannabis company in the state of Florida, the third most populous state in the United States. Its vertically-integrated "seed-to-sale" operation has approximately 50% of the Florida market. With a patient base that grows approximately 10% month-to-month, it is poised for growth in this attractive market. Trulieve boasts over 340+ SKUs [stock keeping units] and is constantly adding new, fresh, and exciting items to its product line. Its widespread dispensary network and large delivery fleet provides important, much-needed access to thousands of patients every day throughout the state. Trulieve is committed to growing its dispensary footprint in the state, constantly identifying new locations that will bring Trulieve closer to patients, allowing many more people to have easier access to the medicine they need. The Company has 45 stores in Florida with more growth ahead. Its first mover advantage in the state provides numerous benefits, including brand recognition and media attention. Strong financial performance, driven by sales to a loyal and dedicated group of patients affectionately called Trulievers, positions the company's commitment to continue its pattern of growth.

Finally, Trulieve is actively expanding outside the state of Florida. The company has already announced purchases of licenses in California, Massachusetts and a dispensary in Connecticut in 2019 and plans to continue its national expansion strategy in 2020.

Source: investors.trulieve.com

Solid

Cresco Labs Inc. (US OTC: CRLBF; TSX: CL)

(Founded 2013; headquartered in Chicago, Illinois)

Cresco Labs has one of the larger distribution networks in the United States with at least 21 dispensaries spread across 11 states. Cresco's main focus is on the American Midwest – with Midwest cannabis sales projected to grow substantially over the next five years. Recreational sales in Cresco's home state of Illinois just began in January 2020. Illinois sales will add substantially to Cresco's numbers. In what was a hot competition for the Illinois recreational market, Cresco won multiple licenses in the Chicago area including two in Chicago's central district and one near Wrigley Field. Many believe Cresco may have the most strategic Illinois retail sales network amongst competitors. Total revenue for 2019 was $128.5 million – an increase of 197% year-over-year. That's the good news.

The bad news is that in Cresco's most recent quarterly results, the company reported a net loss of $45.2 million, widening from a net loss of only $4.4 million a year before. Shortly after, multiple analysts that cover the cannabis space reduced previously aggressive revenue and earnings projections for Cresco. In a move to tighten up the balance sheet, Cresco recently cancelled a pending acquisition for approximately $282.5 million, including approximately $55 million in cash. With the termination of that deal, Cresco has no outstanding acquisitions or other major capital obligations. Cresco's balance sheet is free for continued expansion in Illinois and other Midwestern states. I am expecting improvements. Although not profitable at the moment, Cresco at least has a strong path to profitability in the near future and terrific prospects for continued growth.

Corporate Description

Cresco Labs is one of the largest vertically integrated multi-state cannabis operators in the United States. Cresco is built to become the most important company in the cannabis industry by combining the most strategic geographic footprint with one of the leading distribution platforms in North America. Employing a consumer-packaged goods ("CPG") approach to cannabis, Cresco's house of brands is designed to meet the needs of all consumer segments and includes some of the most recognized and trusted national brands including Cresco, Remedi and Mindy's, a line of edibles created by James Beard Award-winning chef Mindy Segal. Sunnyside, Cresco's national dispensary brand, is a wellness-focused retailer designed to build trust, education and convenience for both existing and new cannabis consumers. Recognizing that the cannabis industry is poised to become one of the leading job creators in the country, Cresco has launched the industry's first national comprehensive Social Equity and Educational Development (SEED) initiative designed to ensure that all members of society have the skills, knowledge and opportunity to work in and own businesses in the cannabis industry.

Source: investors.crescolabs.com/investors/overview

Harvest Health & Recreation Inc. (US OTC: HRVSF; CSE: HARV)

(Founded 2007; headquartered in Tempe, Arizona)

Harvest Health is a mixed bag. They have one of the larger MSO footprints in the United States, but with a more west and southwest focus than some others. They are the market leader in the strong medical marijuana state of Arizona. Like others, Harvest Health has been busy in the merger and acquisition space, but with mixed results. Multiple small acquisitions have led to continued revenue growth, while a couple of larger transactions have been cancelled or otherwise fallen through. In 2020, Harvest announced that it would divest numerous retail locations in California, while claiming they wished to focus on and expand core markets in states such as Arizona, Florida, Maryland, and Pennsylvania. It would maintain a smaller presence in California. The move does give the company extra cash and streamlines operations.

A win for Arizona recreational cannabis sales in November 2020 would be a major victory for Harvest Health in its home state.

Corporate Description

Headquartered in Tempe, Arizona, Harvest Health & Recreation, Inc. is a multi-state cannabis operator (MSO) and vertically-integrated cannabis company. Subject to completion of announced acquisitions, Harvest will have one of the largest footprints in the U.S.

Since 2011, the company has been committed to expanding its Harvest House of Cannabis retail and wholesale presence throughout the U.S., acquiring, creating and growing leading brands for patients and consumers nationally and continuing toward a path of profitable growth. Harvest's mission is to improve lives through the goodness of cannabis and is focused on its vision to become the most valuable cannabis company in the world.

Source: investor.harvesthoc.com/home

Others of Note

MedMen Enterprises Inc. (US OTC: MMNWF; CSE: MMEN)

(Founded 2010; headquartered in Culver City, California)

If you are looking for beautiful, clean stores in high-end locations, and a company that promotes a lifestyle through brand ambassadors and social media influencers, you should love MedMen. Its primary target audience is millennials. Its primary market is California, where it holds 17 licenses. MedMen has prominent stores in downtown Los Angeles, Beverly Hills, and West Hollywood. It has another fancy store in New York's Manhattan. The company has referred to itself as the "Apple Store of Weed." Publications have called it "The Starbucks of Marijuana." MedMen had hopes and dreams of being America's top marijuana retailer and envisioned itself like a fast-growth tech or retail startup success story.

In my opinion, MedMen is a poster child for everything to avoid in cannabis investing. For virtually anything I had to say about other companies' pragmatic or controlled growth, low-cost cultivation, or frugal operations, I could say the opposite about MedMen. The company simply spends much more than it makes. It has had extremely excessive executive compensation, founders with exotic cars and mansions in Los Angeles, and very little cash on the balance sheet. MedMen has also been accused of a very hostile workplace leading to high executive turnover. There are multiple lawsuits. A former company CFO has sued MedMen while accusing the company of its spendthrift ways – among other allegations. In January 2020, MedMen informed many cannabis producers and growers that it would not be able to pay its bills. A few weeks later, the founding CEO stepped down. No matter what steps the company takes to try to clean up its act, my thought on MedMen has always just been – Nope.

Corporate Description

Founded in 2010, MedMen is North America's premium cannabis retailer. Founders Adam Bierman and Andrew Modlin have defined the next generation discovery platform for cannabis and all its benefits. A robust selection of high-quality products, coupled with a team of cannabis-educated associates cement the Company's commitment to providing an unparalleled experience. MedMen believes that a world where cannabis is legal and regulated is safer, healthier and happier.

Source: investors.medmen.com/home

Acreage Holdings, Inc. (US OTC: ACRGF; CSE: ACRG)

(Founded 1989; headquartered in New York, New York)

Acreage is a conundrum. It has cash on the balance sheet and could be a vastly undervalued stock due to its big transaction with Canopy Growth, or it could just be another overvalued, unprofitable cannabis company.

In April 2019, Canada's Canopy Growth reached an agreement to acquire Acreage for $3.4 billion. That is a big number. But there is one big hitch – the deal's competition is dependent on marijuana's legalization at the federal level in the United States. The acquisition price obviously represents a huge premium to Acreage Holdings' current market value. I do not like the odds for a true federal legalization anytime soon. I see better chances for minor legislation in the United States that further reinforces state-level marijuana laws.

Acreage has operations in about 20 states (including pending acquisitions). Like others, it has been aggressive with its acquisitions. With completion of the transactions, Acreage could actually have the largest opportunity among multi-state operators in terms of the number of states with operating licenses, largest total addressable market, and largest serviceable population. In terms of 2019 total revenue, however, it placed well behind many competitors. Acreage Holdings has reported operating losses pretty much continuously, but with the company's far-reaching presence in the United States, it could easily improve financial results as nationwide sales of marijuana continue to grow.

More recently and like some other cannabis operators in 2020 dealing with COVID-19, Acreage Holdings announced it would furlough some employees and close certain facilities. Like Cresco Labs, Acreage has also terminated planned acquisitions in a move to preserve cash.

Corporate Description

Acreage Chairman and CEO Kevin Murphy's 2011 investment in a Maine cannabis license laid the foundation for who we are today. Understanding the plant's power to heal and change the world, and passionate to help lead the movement, "Murph" launched High Street Capital in 2014. In 2017, High Street Capital rebranded as Acreage Holdings and began its transition from an investment vehicle to a leading, vertically integrated multi-state operator.

2019: A Milestone Year

Last year, Acreage cemented its place as a game-changer in the cannabis industry. It started with the broadcast TV rejection of our "Time is Now" Superbowl PSA that called for further cannabis reform. Press and social media coverage of the spot reached billions. In April, we announced our arrangement with Canopy Growth Corporation, setting the stage for a combined global cannabis powerhouse once it's federally permissible for Canopy to acquire our company. Later, we began rolling out our house of brands, a core component of Acreage's product strategy that includes consumer brands like The Botanist and Live Resin Project. Both brands took home honors at the 2019 Emerald Cup, the premier product competition in cannabis.

We expect 2020 to be a record-breaking year for Acreage. With access to unparalleled intellectual property developed in-house and from our arrangement with Canopy Growth Corporation, we look forward to extending the reach of our house of brands throughout the country. The Botanist, Live Resin Project, Natural Wonder, Prime Wellness and Tweed provide us with a diverse array of products and form factors that appeal to consumers across the cannabis spectrum, and we plan to continue developing and releasing additional products that meet their wants and needs.

Source: acreageholdings.com/about-us

Chapter 11
Extraction and Concentrates

"I've got 99 problems and CBD oil solved like 86 of them."

—Unknown

A mong cannabis sales worldwide, transactions for dried cannabis flower still dominate the market. But cannabis extract in various forms make up the fastest-growing segment of the worldwide cannabis industry. Extracted products such as edibles, beverages, and oil concentrates provide alternatives to smokable cannabis flower. Alternative cannabis products open marketing to a large audience of consumers that may not consider cannabis in its smokable form.

Extraction equipment is highly specialized and the process complicated. Quality and purity are paramount. An increasing number of cannabis companies turn to chemical extraction specialist firms as a means of harvesting the raw materials to manufacture derivative products – whether CBD based, or THC infused. Extraction companies typically enter into multi-year agreements with cannabis firms for product quantity and date deliverables, providing attractive predictable future cash flows.

As compared to the most prominent Canadian LPs and US multi-state operators, the extraction specialists that I will highlight remain relatively small with market capitalizations each in the ballpark of $200 million as of early 2020.

The Best

Valens GroWorks Corp. (US OTC: VLNCF; TSXV: VLNS)

(Founded 1981; headquartered in Kelowna, Canada)

Valens has recently rebranded itself as The Valens Company. It is the largest third-party extraction company in Canada. Valens has agreements with the major Canadian LPs Canopy Growth, Tilray, Organigram, Green Organic Dutchman, and HEXO. With Canada's cannabis 2.0 product sales only getting started in early 2020, Valens is already in a dominant position. Canadian derivative cannabis product sales of edibles and extracts are expected to explode.

Annual capacity is already 425,000 kg (or 936,965 pounds) of dried cannabis and hemp biomass. Valens is in the process of increasing its extraction capacity to 1,000,000 kg (2,204,623 pounds) in 2020.

Corporate Description

The Valens Company is a global leader in the end-to-end development and manufacturing of innovative, cannabinoid-based products. The Company is focused on being the partner of choice for leading Canadian and international cannabis brands by providing best-in-class, proprietary services including CO_2, ethanol, hydrocarbon, solvent-less and terpene extraction, analytical testing, formulation and white label product development and manufacturing. Valens is the largest third-party extraction Company in Canada with an annual capacity of 425,000 kg of dried cannabis and hemp biomass at our purpose-built facility in Kelowna, British Columbia, which is in the process of becoming European Union (EU) Good Manufacturing Practices (GMP) compliant. The Valens Company currently offers a wide range of product formats, including tinctures, two-piece caps, soft gels, oral sprays and vape *pens as well as beverages, concentrates, topicals, edibles, injectables, natural health products and has a strong pipeline of next generation products in development for future release. Finally, the Company's wholly owned subsidiary Valens Labs is a Health Canada licensed ISO 17025 accredited cannabis testing lab providing sector-leading analytical services and has partnered with Thermo Fisher Scientific to develop a Centre of Excellence in Plant-Based Science.*

Source: thevalenscompany.com/investors

MediPharm Labs Corporation (US OTC: MEDIF; TSX: LABS)

(Founded 2015; headquartered in Barrie, Canada)

MediPharm Labs Corp. was the first LP licensed under Canada's ACMPR (Access to Cannabis for Medicinal Purposes Regulations) to focus exclusively on cannabis oil extraction. Medipharm Labs (LABS) is a leader in specialized cannabis extraction, distillation, purification, and cannabinoid isolation. Like Valens, LABS is set to profit from the expected surge in Canadian extracted product sales by being an extraction early mover. It has deals in place with Canopy Growth, Supreme Cannabis, Emerald Health Therapeutics, and others.

MediPharm is also realizing solid growth with both its MediPharm Labs Australia subsidiary and its ability to complete white label supply agreements for cannabis-related finished products.

Corporate Description

MediPharm Labs brings a pharmaceutical perspective to the cannabis industry, working to internationally recognized pharma-quality standards which result in products that are pure, trusted, and precisely dosable for patients and end consumers.

Founded in 2015, MediPharm Labs specializes in the production of purified, pharmaceutical quality cannabis oil and concentrates and advanced derivative products utilizing a Good Manufacturing Practices certified facility with ISO standard-built clean rooms.

MediPharm Labs has invested in an expert, research driven team, state-of-the-art technology, downstream purification methodologies and purpose-built facilities with five primary extraction lines for delivery of pure, trusted and precision-dosed cannabis products for its customers. Through its wholesale and white label platforms, they formulate, consumer-test, process, package and distribute cannabis extracts and advanced cannabinoid-based products to domestic and international markets. As a global leader, MediPharm Labs has completed commercial exports to Australia and is nearing commercialization of its Australian Extraction facility. MediPharm Labs Australia was established in 2017.

Source: medipharmlabs.com/about-us

Others of Note

Neptune Wellness Solutions, Inc. (NASDAQ: NEPT; TSX: NEPT)

(Founded 1998; headquartered in Laval, Canada)

Neptune Wellness has a strong position in North America with both Canadian and US (hemp / CBD only) operations. While competitors Valens and Medipharm Labs remain only Toronto-listed (while also traded OTC in the United States), Neptune has the added benefit of a United States Nasdaq listing. The company had years of experience in wellness products, including fish oils, seed oils, pet supplements, and topicals; but just received its license to process cannabis from Health Canada in January 2019. In addition to its Quebec, Canada, facilities, the company operates in Conover, North Carolina, where it processes hemp biomass. Its North Carolina facility is expected to reach an annual capacity of 1,500,000 kg. Combined extraction capacity between United States and Canadian operations should exceed 3,000,000 kg per year under currently planned expansions.

Corporate Description

Neptune Wellness Solutions is a Leader in Three Main Areas
Cannabis and Industrial Hemp Extraction

We operate in the Canadian cannabis, global medical cannabis and hemp industries. At our Canadian facility, we focus on the extraction, purification and formulation of cannabis products.

In the U.S., our Sugarleaf Labs facility offers high-quality full and broad-spectrum industrial hemp products. Starting from the highest-quality American-grown hemp, we incorporate sophisticated manufacturing practices to retain the natural qualities of the plant in the extracts we produce.

Turnkey Solutions

Nutrition Products. We specialize in the development and commercialization of turnkey supplements in various delivery forms. We source the finest ingredients from verified suppliers or formulate using our proprietary, branded ingredients to create ideal products that are ready for sale under our customers' brand.

Pet Supplements. Comprising superior ingredients, our 100% natural and scientifically formulated pet supplements offer human-grade quality ingredients in a variety of concentrations.

Consumer Brands

Forest Remedies. We produce high-quality hemp-derived products from hemp that is grown exclusively in the U.S. We are involved in every part of the process of making our own finished products, from working with the farmers during the growth cycle to processing, formulating, testing, packaging and distributing a consumer-ready product to our customers. Our products are available to consumers in the U.S.

Ocean Remedies. Ocean Remedies' mission is to promote sustainable, marine-based supplements that support healthy people and ecosystems while delivering access and life-changing vitamins to people in need. Ocean Remedies products are available to consumers in the U.S. for direct purchase.

OCEANO3. Made from Antarctic krill, a sustainable and non-genetically-modified source of omega-3 fatty acids, our OCEANO3 Krill Oil is available to consumers in Canada for direct purchase or to distributors as a wholesale opportunity.

Source: neptunecorp.com/who-we-are

Chapter 12
Hemp and CBD Focused

"Make the most you can of the Indian Hemp seed and sow it everywhere."

– George Washington

D ue to the current status of federal laws in the United States, we have a very clear distinction between legal CBD-only product producers and federally illegal, marijuana cultivating multi-state operators. For investors, a question remains about how much upside growth the US CBD market has as compared to the overall cannabis market with continued advancement in cannabis legislation.

CBD product sales exploded on the scene in the United States following hemp's inclusion in the Farm Bill of 2018. Specifically, for the first time in decades, US legislation would define hemp as the cannabis plant but that cannot contain more than 0.3% of THC. The Farm Bill did not actually legalize CBD, but through the Farm Bill's passage, proper CBD could be. Cannabinoid must be specifically derived from hemp that is produced in a manner consistent with the Farm Bill, associated federal regulations, associated state regulations, and by a licensed grower. That Farm Bill also stated that the US Food and Drug Administration (FDA) would have oversight.

In just the short period of time since that Farm Bill passed, dozens of large traditional retailers have added the sale of CBD products, including major pharmacies like CVS, Rite-Aid, and Walgreens, grocers such as Kroger, specialty stores like The Vitamin Shoppe, and convenience stores from coast to coast. However, state laws still vary greatly. Some state laws allow CBD sales. Some states prohibit all CBD sales. Some states allow CBD sales with certain labeling requirements. Other states are operating in the regulatory gray area in between. Much remains to be sorted out in the regulatory framework surrounding CBD.

In late 2019 and early 2020, the FDA began issuing warning letters to companies illegally selling unapproved products that allegedly contain cannabidiol (CBD), or marketing products using unsubstantiated claims regarding the potential health benefits of CBD. The FDA also sent out a press release warning consumers that CBD can have negative health consequences. While the FDA has pledged action against unlawful CBD products, the agency's new commissioner Stephen Hahn appointed in December 2019 has expressed support for CBD products. In a public speech, Hahn stated, "People are using these products. We're not going to be able to say you can't use these products. It's a fool's game to try to even approach that."

Much remains to be clarified. The FDA has announced that it is actively exploring pathways to allow for the marketing of cannabidiol as a dietary supplement and is developing enforcement guidance. The agency has asked the industry to collaborate with the government in the study of CBD's possible benefits and dangers.

The largest makers of legal, high-quality CBD products are in full agreement with the FDA's stance on unsubstantiated product claims but would like CBD rules and regulations clarified as soon as possible. A clear regulatory environment for CBD will only serve as a boost for the larger, publicly traded, and legal product producers by helping to stamp out small competitors that operate on the fringes of legality while making crazy claims of CBD benefits. With clear regulations, the legitimate CBD firms can greatly increase CBD partnerships and marketing to grab dominant market share.

The Best

Charlotte's Web Holdings, Inc. (US OCT: CWBHF; TSX: CWEB)

(Founded 2011; headquartered in Boulder, Colorado)

Charlotte's Web has a great story that helped it quickly gain a leadership position among US CBD providers. With the original name Stanley Brothers, the company changed the firm's name in honor of the young girl Charlotte Figi, suffering from Dravet syndrome, a rare form of epilepsy that was not controlled by traditional medication. Charlotte's story was covered extensively by CNN Chief Medical Correspondent Dr. Sanjay Gupta in the documentary *Weed*. The Stanley Brothers' low THC, high CBD strain of cannabis oil is credited with largely eliminating her epileptic symptoms after all other pharmaceutical avenues had been exhausted.

If you strongly believe in the expansion of the CBD-only product market, Charlotte's Web is already in the driver's seat. The company had a market capitalization of close to $500 million in early 2020 – far ahead of other CBD competitors. CWEB has built out a retail presence wider than that of its competitors with products found in at least 11,000 stores across the United States, including retail giants like CVS Health. With the acquisition of CBD competitor Abacus Health announced in March 2020, the combined company would have a presence in at least 15,000 retail locations and cover at least 35% of the nationwide market share for CBD products.

The company is currently building a 137,000-square-foot production facility in Colorado. The facility should be operational by the end of 2020 and will increase Charlotte's Web's production capabilities tenfold.

Corporate Description

Charlotte's Web, founded by the Stanley Brothers, is an industry-leading pioneer creating whole-plant hemp health supplements. A vertically integrated company, every step of the process is overseen to ensure the highest quality, from seed to self.

At Charlotte's Web our mission is to improve life, naturally. We do this by responsibly growing our proprietary non-GMO hemp genetics on family farms that are made into premium, full-spectrum phytocannabinoid health and wellness products. Charlotte's Web is manufactured in an FDA-registered facility and 3rd party-verified for Good Manufacturing Practices.

The Stanley brothers from Colorado – Joel, Jesse, Jared, Josh, Jordan, Jon, and Austin – have tapped into their rugged roots and connection to botanical medicine to become pioneers and leaders in the cannabis industry.

The brothers have helped to transform laws and thousands of lives through their social enterprise companies that dive into uncharted territories of plant-based science and health.

Their groundbreaking innovation, Charlotte's Web, is named for little Charlotte Figi, whose remarkable story with the brothers received global media recognition.

As their journey continues, the brothers are collaborating with prestigious research institutions, thought-leaders, non-profits, and governments to advance cannabinoid research, policy and education.

Source: investors.charlottesweb.com/our-company

cbdMD, Inc. (NYSE American: YCBD)

(Founded 2015; headquartered in Charlotte, North Carolina)

If Charlotte's Web is the CBD market leader, cbdMD is the clear number two. It's still a small firm with market capitalization around $50 million in early 2020, but it's quickly building brand recognition. The company markets under two CBD brands in America: cbdMD and Paw CBD. The company was formerly known as Level Brands, Inc. and only formed under the brand name cbdMD, Inc. in May 2019. cbdMD touts CBD purity that is 100% THC free and uses a large stable of professional athletes – athletes that must regularly pass sport related drug tests – as brand ambassadors.

While the company has reported all net losses so far, it should continue growth and could get a good boost with FDA clarity on CBD regulation. cbdMD has a solid balance sheet following a

January 2020 stock offering. While the issuance of additional shares temporarily dinged YCBD's stock price, raising capital turned out to be a brilliant move just before the COVID19 pandemic truly hit the country.

According to company releases, approximately 67% of the firm's total sales are through its e-commerce channel, with 33% through over 5,300 retail stores. cbdMD and Paw CBD also sell to wholesale customers in 16 international markets.

Corporate Description

Here at cbdMD, we pride ourselves on two things: quality and innovation.

Our goal has always been to produce the industry's absolute highest-quality CBD while using state-of-the-art production and manufacturing techniques.

Take the highest-quality hemp, combined with the industry's most sophisticated manufacturing methods, and it's obvious why our CBD oil is the first choice for a wide range of people looking for natural support.

There's a huge difference in CBD produced in the United States compared to CBD produced abroad. We spare no expense when it comes to ensuring the quality of our CBD – we take pride in our commitment to providing premium-quality CBD manufactured domestically in the USA. We guarantee your complete satisfaction or your money back.

Our primary goal has always been consistently to deliver the absolute highest-quality CBD in the industry. When manufacturing CBD from hemp, there are several methods available.

Though very expensive, our manufacturing process is the only viable option for preserving all the valuable properties of the hemp plant, not just some – while eliminating the presence of THC.

Having invested in some of the industry's most sophisticated technology, our laboratory can produce high-quality CBD consistently. By continuing to develop and research proper production strategies, we're able to save the powerful properties of the hemp plant so you can enjoy a naturally better product.

Our CBD undergoes rigorous testing throughout the entire manufacturing and production process to ensure nothing but high-quality CBD oil in every batch. Our products further undergo additional and extensive third-party testing through independent labs so we can confidently guarantee our products are free of synthetic additives. We pride ourselves on being fully transparent and welcome you to view the independent third-party testing results.

Source: cbdmd.com/about-cbdmd

Others of Note

CV Sciences, Inc. (US OTC: CVSI)

(Founded 2010; headquartered in San Diego, California)

CV Sciences remains a small over-the-counter (OTC) traded stock rather than listing on an exchange in either Canada or the United States. It trades for well under $1, as of mid-2020.

With only a handful of real market leaders in the CBD space, CVSI has made its name for itself through its PlusCBD Oil brand. It is available in at least 3,000 retail outlets across the United States. It is a firm to keep an eye on for the future with CBD expansion or if it becomes an exchange listed security. The company could otherwise be an acquisition target.

Corporate Description

CV Sciences, Inc. operates two distinct business segments: a consumer product division focused on manufacturing, marketing and selling plant-based CBD products to a range of market sectors; and a drug development division focused on developing and commercializing CBD-based novel therapeutics utilizing CBD. The Company's PlusCBD™ Oil is the top-selling brand of hemp-derived CBD on the market, according to SPINS, the leading provider of syndicated data and insights for the natural, organic and specialty products industry. CV Sciences' state-of-the-art facility follows all guidelines for Good Manufacturing Practices (GMP) and the Company's full spectrum hemp extracts are processed, produced, and tested throughout the manufacturing process to confirm the cannabinoid content meets strict company standards. With a commitment to science, PlusCBD™ Oil was the first hemp CBD supplement brand to invest in the scientific evidence necessary to receive self-affirmed Generally Recognized as Safe (GRAS) status. CV Sciences, Inc. has primary offices and facilities in San Diego, California.

Source: cvsciences.com

Chapter 13
Pharmaceutical and Biotech

"Since 1999, opioid overdose deaths have quadrupled and opioid prescriptions have increased markedly – almost enough for every adult in America to have a bottle of pills."
— US Surgeon General Vivik Murthy

The development of cannabis-based medicines and the further expansion of medical marijuana use has the potential to cannibalize current spending on numerous medical conditions. Studies have found that the use of traditional prescription drugs fell in states where medical marijuana had been legalized. But beyond the use of medical marijuana, research related to the medical applications of cannabinoids can lead to the development of new cannabis-based drugs and uncover new uses for derivatives of the cannabis plant. According to a 2017 study by the National Academies of Science, cannabis and related products could be effective in treating chronic pain, PTSD, sleep disorders, anxiety, nerve pain, chemotherapy-induced nausea and vomiting, Tourette syndrome, and multiple sclerosis-related spasticity among other conditions.[1]

The existing opioid market could face the greatest cannibalization risk from cannabis-based medicines and medical marijuana.

According to Grand View Research, the current global market for opioids is worth about $23 billion and is expected to grow to almost $35 billion by the year 2025.[2] North America and its rising geriatric population accounts for more than half of the global opioid total. Opioid use has come under intense scrutiny due to the overly large number of the overdose deaths. The abuse of opioids has become a national crisis. According to the CDC (Centers for Disease Control and Prevention), more than 67,000 people died in the United States from drug overdose in 2018. Opioids were by far the worst culprit. Cannabis may offer a solution to North America's opioid epidemic.

The Best

GW Pharmaceuticals plc (NASDAQ: GWPH)

(Founded 1998; headquartered in Cambridge, United Kingdom)

Britain's GW Pharmaceuticals is a clear leader as a cannabis-focused biopharmaceutical company, having developed and commercialized cannabinoid prescription medicines from extracts of the cannabis plant. Its lead product is Epidiolex, an oral medicine for the treatment of refractory childhood epilepsies, as well as for the treatment of Dravet syndrome, Lennox-Gastaut syndrome, tuberous sclerosis complex, and infantile spasms. It is a large company of over $3 billion in market capitalization and NASDAQ-listed. It may be the most widely accepted cannabis company in the world. It is a firm that actually handles marijuana plants but is recognized as a fully legal pharmaceutical drug manufacturer whose stock is widely held by exchange-traded funds, pensions, and other institutional accounts. GW holds license and development agreements with numerous healthcare companies and drug developers Almirall SA; Bayer HealthCare AG; Ipsen Biopharm Ltd.; and Neopharm Group. It is a true multinational company operating in the United Kingdom, Europe, Canada, Asia, and the United States.

Corporate Description

GW was co-founded in 1998 by Dr. Geoffrey Guy and Dr. Brian Whittle, two well-known entrepreneurs in the UK biotech sector. In setting up GW, Drs. Guy and Whittle worked closely with both the UK Home Office and the UK's medicines regulatory authority on establishing necessary licenses and procedures so as to facilitate the progress of GW's cannabinoid research program.

In 1999, GW commenced its first clinical trials evaluating different cannabinoid formulations as potential therapeutics with an initial focus on the development of an oral mucosal spray of a complex botanical mixture comprised of two principal cannabinoid components, cannabidiol (CBD) and delta-9 tetrahydrocannabinol (THC), along with specific minor cannabinoids and non-cannabinoid plant components.

Working with leading cannabinoid scientists around the world, GW has continued to explore the potential of a range of novel cannabinoid molecules in a number of distinct therapeutic areas including epilepsy, glioma, and schizophrenia.

GW's lead product is a liquid formulation of highly purified CBD. In June 2018, the FDA approved this product as EPIDIOLEX® (cannabidiol) for the treatment of seizures associated with Lennox-Gastaut syndrome (LGS) or Dravet syndrome, two rare and particularly difficult to treat forms of epilepsy, in patients 2 years and older and the DEA designated it as a Schedule V controlled substance, the least restrictive schedule. The product was launched in November 2018 and is now available by prescription only in the U.S.

This product also received approval in the EU by the European Medicines Agency (EMA) under the tradename EPIDYOLEX® for use as adjunctive therapy of seizures associated with Lennox Gastaut syndrome (LGS) or Dravet syndrome, in conjunction with clobazam, for patients 2 years of age and older. GW is currently evaluating additional clinical development programs in other orphan seizure disorders and autism spectrum disorders.

GW's focus is to bring novel, cannabinoid-based prescription medicines to patients in areas of serious unmet need and in which our medicines have the potential to make a real difference to their quality of life.

Source: gwpharm.com/about/history

Corbus Pharmaceuticals Holdings, Inc. (NASDAQ: CRBP)

(Founded 2009; headquartered in Norwood, Massachusetts)

Smaller than GW Pharmaceuticals, Corbus is still a good sized, NASDAQ-listed pharmaceutical company. The company prides itself on being smaller and more nimble than typical Big Pharma. Corbus is still a clinical-stage pharmaceutical company, rather than having drugs in the market. Its focus on the development of synthetic cannabinoid-based drugs could lead to serious breakthroughs with the ability to surpass GW's naturally derived cannabinoid medicines. As a pharmaceutical drug maker working with synthetic non-psychoactive cannabinoids, Corbus has no worries about US federal legality. It doesn't touch marijuana plants.

Corporate Description

Corbus Pharmaceuticals Holdings, Inc. is a Phase 3 clinical-stage pharmaceutical company focused on the development and commercialization of novel therapeutics to treat inflammatory and fibrotic diseases by leveraging its pipeline of rationally designed, endocannabinoid system-targeting drug candidates. The Company's lead product candidate, lenabasum, is a novel, oral, selective cannabinoid receptor type 2 (CB2) agonist rationally designed to resolve chronic inflammation and fibrotic processes. Lenabasum is currently being evaluated in systemic sclerosis, cystic fibrosis, dermatomyositis and systemic lupus erythematosus.

Corbus is also developing a pipeline of drug candidates targeting the endocannabinoid system. The pipeline includes CRB-4001, a 2nd generation, selective cannabinoid receptor type 1 (CB1) inverse agonist designed to be peripherally restricted. Potential indications for CRB-4001 include nonalcoholic steatohepatitis (NASH), among others. Corbus expects data from its Phase 1 safety study in 2020.

Source: corbuspharma.com/our-company/overview

Zynerba Pharmaceuticals, Inc. (NASDAQ: ZYNE)

(Founded 2007; headquartered in Devon, Pennsylvania)

NASDAQ-listed Zynerba is another clinical stage specialty pharmaceutical company. It is a smaller company with a market cap around $100 million, but like Corbus it works with synthetically produced cannabinoids. Zynerba focuses on developing transdermal (absorbed through the skin) cannabinoid therapies. The company's leading developmental product is Zygel, a transdermal cannabidiol gel in clinic trials for the treatment of children and adolescent patients with rare epilepsies, fragile X syndrome, and autism spectrum disorder among other potential uses. The company is definitely working on good things.

Corporate Description

Zynerba is dedicated to improving the lives of people with rare and near rare neuropsychiatric disorders where there is a high unmet medical need by pioneering the development and commercialization of next-generation pharmaceutically-produced cannabinoid therapeutics formulated for transdermal delivery. Cannabinoids interact with specific receptors throughout the body to produce pharmacologic effects, primarily in the CNS and immune systems.

Zynerba's lead patent-protected product candidate in clinical development is Zygel™. Zygel is the first and only pharmaceutically produced cannabidiol (CBD) formulated as a permeation-enhanced gel for transdermal delivery. Through a proprietary combination of our pharmaceutically-produced CBD and permeation enhancers, we believe we can effectively deliver CBD through the layers of the epidermis and into the circulatory system. The company is currently assessing Zygel in Fragile X Syndrome, Autism Spectrum Disorder, a rare genetic neuropsychiatric syndrome called 22q11.2 Deletion Syndrome, and a heterogeneous group of rare and ultra-rare epilepsy syndromes associated with severe cognitive impairment and behavioral disturbances known as developmental and epileptic encephalopathies (DEE).

Cannabinoids appear to modulate a number of systems, channels and receptors; as such, they may have the potential to be developed in a number of additional important indications, including anxiety, autism spectrum disorder, neuroprotection, cognitive disorders, sleep disturbance, and treatment for certain neuralgias.

Zynerba is the leader in pharmaceutically produced transdermal cannabinoid therapies for rare and near-rare neuropsychiatric disorders. Zynerba is developing a compelling wholly owned clinical pipeline that may address significant unmet medical needs. Currently Zygel is patent protected through 2030, and the Company continually seeks to augment patent protection and explore other opportunities for exclusivity. For example, the US Food and Drug Administration has granted Zynerba Orphan Drug designation for the use of CBD as treatment for Fragile X Syndrome, which among other incentives, may provide market exclusivity in the approved indication for a period of seven years.

Source: ir.zynerba.com/corporate-profile

Cardiol Therapeutics Inc. (US OTC: CRTPF; TSX: CRDL)

(Founded 2017; headquartered in Oakville, Canada)

Cardiol is Canadian-based, but like Corbus and Zynerba, is doing excellent work with pharmaceutically developed cannabinoids. Still a very small company with a market capitalization around $50–60 million in early 2020, it could offer terrific upside.

In addition to producing their own synthetic CBD products, Cardiol is also developing various therapies for heart diseases as well as proprietary nanotechnologies that would deliver pharmaceutical CBD and other anti-inflammatories directly to the heart. It's exciting stuff.

Corporate Description

The Company is focused on producing pharmaceutical cannabidiol ("CBD") products and developing innovative therapies for heart disease, including acute myocarditis and other causes of heart failure.

We are leveraging our expertise in pharmaceutical cannabinoids to develop proprietary formulations for commercial development in two important medical markets: commercializing a line of pharmaceutical cannabidiol products in the growing market for medical cannabinoids and developing nanotechnologies designed to deliver cannabinoids and other anti-inflammatory drugs to the heart for the treatment of inflammatory heart disease.

Our lead product, CardiolRxTM, is designed to be the safest and most consistent cannabidiol formulation on the market. CardiolRxTM is pharmaceutically produced, cGMP certified, and is THC free (<5 ppm). We plan to commercialize CardiolRxTM in the *billion-dollar market for medicinal cannabinoids in Canada and we will be pursuing market introduction opportunities in Europe and Latin America.*

Cardiol is planning an international clinical study of Cardiol-RxTM in acute myocarditis, a condition caused by inflammation in heart tissue, which remains the most common cause of sudden cardiac death in people less than 35 years of age and is a common cause of acute heart failure.

We are also developing proprietary nanotechnology to deliver pharmaceutical cannabidiol and other anti-inflammatory drugs directly to sites of inflammation in the heart that are associated with the development and progression of heart failure.

The Company has research programs focused on developing nanotherapeutics to treat heart failure underway at international centers of excellence, including the University of Alberta, the Houston Methodist DeBakey Heart & Vascular Center, and TecSalud del Tecnológico de Monterrey ("TecSalud").

Cardiol has also established an exclusive manufacturing arrangement with Dalton Pharma Services, a Health Canada-approved, U.S. Food and Drug Administration ("FDA") registered, Current Good Manufacturing Practice ("cGMP") manufacturer of pharmaceuticals, including cannabinoids, for supplying finished pharmaceutically produced cannabidiol products to support the Corporation's research and commercial development programs.

Source: cardiolrx.com/about-us/company-overview

Cannabis Is Not Their Main Business

Arena Pharmaceuticals, Inc. (NASDAQ: ARNA)

(Founded 1997; headquartered in San Diego, California)

Arena is a sizable, mid-cap biopharmaceutical company that is worth about $2.5 billion. It shows up on lists of cannabis-related companies but is far from a marijuana stock. Arena is well diversified with multiple drug candidates in the pipeline. While Arena has other non-cannabinoid drugs further along in approval stage, one particularly exciting candidate is a clinical-stage oral medication that targets the cannabinoid receptor system with the goal of replacing opioid therapies.

AbbVie Inc. Name (NYSE: ABBV)

(Founded 2012; headquartered in North Chicago, Illinois)

AbbVie is a very large biopharmaceutical company that develops and markets products in the United States, Japan, Germany, Canada, France, Spain, Italy, the Netherlands, the United Kingdom, Brazil, and internationally. They have a market capitalization of over $125 billion. The company's main revenue drug is the massive seller HUMIRA.

People like to consider Abbvie a cannabis-related company since it brought Marinol to market, a synthetic cannabis-based drug. Marinol (dronabinol) is a prescription medicine that can be used to treat nausea caused by chemotherapy and a loss of appetite in people who have lost weight due to HIV-related conditions. It's a very small part of what Abbvie does.

Novartis AG (NYSE: NVS)

(Founded 1895; headquartered in Basel, Switzerland)

Novartis is a true multinational pharmaceutical powerhouse. As of early 2020, it has a market capitalization of nearly $200 billion. They research, develop, manufacture, and sell healthcare products worldwide. Cannabis is certainly not their focus, but they are an excellent company to partner with.

In December 2018, Novartis subsidiary Sandoz signed an agreement with the Canadian LP Tilray to sell medical marijuana in countries around the world where it is legal. Novartis and Sandoz have fantastic international reach and leverage. Their agreement also calls for the two companies to jointly develop new derivative cannabis products such as edibles, topicals, and sprays.

Catalent, Inc. (NYSE: CTLT)

(Founded 2007; headquartered in Somerset, New Jersey)

Healthcare company Catalent, like many large multinational pharmaceutical companies, has a DEA license to handle marijuana legally. With a market cap of over $10 billion, they are a leader in drug delivery technologies and manufacturing solutions –meaning they primarily partner with others to provide services in drug development.

Catalent has a US DEA registered facility in Missouri for the import of cannabis extracts in dosage form for clinical trial studies. They also partnered with the Calgary-based pharmaceutical company Ethicann to use botanically sourced cannabinoid oils in the development of new prescription drugs. The partnership plans to use Catalent's orally disintegrating tablet technology to develop a new combination pharmaceutical-grade CBD and THC product that could treat patients suffering from multiple sclerosis spasticity.

Like Arena, AbbVie, or Novartis, Catalent, is an excellent company with cannabis exposure, but a company that should be considered under its primary business lines – not particularly as a cannabis-focused investment.

Notes

1. Wright, P. (2019). Cannabis industry primer: Growing like a weed. *Intro Blue*, May 23.
2. Wright, P. (2019). Cannabis industry primer: Growing like a weed. *Intro Blue*, May 23.

Chapter 14
Suppliers and Everyone Else

"During the Gold Rush, most would-be miners lost money, but people who sold them picks, shovels, tents and blue-jeans made a nice profit."

—Peter Lynch

Sometimes called "pick and shovel" investments based on the stories of 1849's Gold Rush; ancillary companies that service another industry can make for smart investments. As compared to the major Canadian licensed producers and United States multi-state operators that actually cultivate, market, and sell cannabis, the pick and shovel companies that specialize in cannabis-related business are often smaller stocks with lighter trading volume. They depend on the success of cannabis expansion and can be quite volatile – just like all of the cannabis industry. Ancillary companies should take only an ancillary role in an investment portfolio.

The Best

GrowGeneration Corp. (NASDAQ: GRWG)

(Founded 2008; headquartered in Denver, Colorado)

US hydroponic growth company GrowGeneration just listed on the NASDAQ exchange in December 2019 after being in business since 2008. The company operates in at least 10 states and is close to $200 million in market capitalization as of early 2020. The company operates organic growth stores and sells nutrients, soils, and advanced lighting technology for commercial growers. The company is still relatively small but is in fast growth mode as a corporation. As a leader in its unique space, it has great room for continued expansion along with the overall cannabis market.

Corporate Description

GrowGeneration Corp. ("GrowGen") is currently the largest hydroponic equipment supplier in the country, with 27 organic garden centers, across 10 states. We carry and sell thousands of products, from organic nutrients, soils, advanced lighting technology, to state-of-the-art hydroponic equipment used by commercial and home growers. Additionally, we carry propagation supplies, pest controls, environmental controllers and ventilation solutions. With a dedicated professional growing staff, we aim to service any size grow in order to lower costs, maximize yield, and provide facility or project consultations. We also offer greenhouse design solutions and harvesting solutions at any scale. Our team of experts are on call 24/7 to assist all growers.

Our story began in Pueblo, Colorado in 2014. Pueblo Organics and Hydroponics was the first location that GrowGeneration acquired, which laid the foundation and allowed our team to develop the company into what it is today. With only a handful of employees, the team began opening locations in Conifer, Denver, and Trinidad only to soon relocate the headquarters to Denver, Colorado. This was the first phase of expansion. Over the last 5 years GrowGeneration has opened or acquired a total of 24 locations starting in Colorado and headed west to Nevada, California and Washington, only to make way back east into Oklahoma, Michigan, Rhode Island, Maine, and New Hampshire.

GrowGeneration Corp. is publicly traded on NASDAQ. The stock symbol is GRWG. Management estimates that roughly 1,000 hydroponic stores are in operation in the U.S. By 2020, the market is estimated to reach over $23 billion with a compound annual growth rate of 32%.

Source: growgeneration.com/about

Greenlane Holdings, Inc. (NASDAQ: GNLN)

(Founded 2005; headquartered in Boca Raton, Florida)

As is true with some other cannabis-related companies that don't actually cultivate or sell, marijuana, Greenlane is a federally legal retailer of cannabis accessories and is listed on the NASDAQ exchange. It is still a tiny company by market cap. Just like other stocks associated with cannabis, Greenlane's stock price has suffered through 2019. With the company's expansion across the United States and Canada, expenses increased. Sales revenue took a serious hit with the vape crisis in 2019, practically shutting down one of Greenlane's main product lines. As I have stated before, vape-related health problems were really related to illegal, black market products but devastated the sale of vape products across the board. With vape negativity behind it and a strong retail presence in the cannabis universe, Greenlane could offer great upside potential from its current stock price.

Corporate Description

Greenlane is one of the largest global sellers of premium cannabis accessories, CBD and liquid nicotine products. The Company operates as a powerful house of brands, third party brand accelerator and distribution platform for consumption devices and lifestyle brands serving the global cannabis, CBD, and liquid nicotine markets with an expansive customer base of more than 11,000 retail locations, including licensed cannabis dispensaries, and smoke and vape shops. Greenlane has an established track record of partnering with brands through all stages of product lifecycle, providing a range of services including product development, go-to-market strategy, sales and marketing support, market research, customer service, direct-to-consumer fulfillment, warranty repair, supply chain management, and distribution. In addition to owning and operating its own brands, Greenlane is the partner of choice for many of the industry's leading players including PAX Labs, (Canopy-owned) Storz & Bickel, JUUL, Grenco Science, Firefly, DaVinci, Select, Sherbinski, Bloom Farms, Mary's Nutritionals, Cookies and dozens of others. Greenlane's house of brands is comprised of child-resistant packaging innovator Pollen Gear; VIBES rolling papers; the Marley Natural accessory line; the Keith Haring accessory line, Aerospaced & Groove grinders, and Higher Standards, which is both an upscale product line and an innovative retail experience with flagship stores at New York City's famed Chelsea Market and Atlanta's Ponce City Market. The company also owns and operates Vapor.com, *an industry leading e-commerce platform which offers convenient, flexible shopping solutions directly to consumers.*

Source: gnln.com/greenlane-distribution

Others of Note

KushCo Holdings, Inc. (US OTC: KSHB)

(Founded 2010; headquartered in Cypress, California)

Kush is still a relatively small over-the-counter (OTC) traded stock not yet listed on an exchange in Canada or the US, although it is a fairly famous name in the world of cannabis. Its total size is around $75 million as of early 2020 and trades well under $1 per share. It had priced for more than $6 per share in January 2019. Kush has continually expanded beyond just cannabis accessories and packaging solutions into vaporizer hardware and technology, hydrocarbons and solvents for cannabis extraction, retail services to CBD businesses, and even hemp commodity trading. Like Greenlane Holdings, Kush's stock price suffered with the so-called vaping crisis and with expenses exceeding revenues.

Corporate Description

KushCo Holdings, Inc. is a publicly traded company and the parent company to a diverse group of business units that are transformative leaders in the cannabis and CBD industries. Our subsidiaries provide exceptional customer service, product quality, compliancy knowledge and a local presence in serving its diverse customer base.

Our brands include Kush Supply Co., the nation's largest, most respected and premier provider of vaporizer products, packaging, supplies, and accessories; Kush Energy, a provider of ultra-pure hydrocarbon gases and solvents to the cannabis and CBD industries; The Hybrid Creative, a premier creative design agency for cannabis and non-cannabis brands; and, Koleto Innovations, our research and development arm driving intellectual property development and acquisitions.

Founded in 2010, KushCo has now sold more than 1 billion units and regularly services more than 6,000 legally operated medical and adult-use growers, processors, and producers across North America, South America, and Europe. We maintain facilities in the five largest U.S. cannabis markets and we have a local sales presence in every major cannabis market across the US and Canada.

KushCo strives to be the industry leader for responsible and compliant products and services in the cannabis and CBD industries. While KushCo services all facets of the cannabis industry, it has no direct involvement with the cannabis plant or any products that contain THC.

Source: ir.kushco.com/company-information

Akerna Corp. (NASDAQ: KERN)

(Founded 2010; headquartered in Orlando, Florida)

Akerna is an interesting play between two fast-growth industries – cloud software and cannabis. The firm provides end-to-end management tracking systems for licensed dispensaries, cultivators, product manufacturers, and distributors. It is specialized for legal compliance in the cannabis industry. The company is still small, with a market cap of less than $100 million. The stock has been volatile right along with the cannabis industry, but also may carry tremendous upside along with overall industry growth.

Corporate Description

Akerna is the parent company resulting from the merger between MJ Freeway and MTech Acquisition Corp., the first US-listed Special Purpose Acquisition Company (SPAC) focused on acquiring a cannabis technology company. Akerna has acquired cash proceeds released from MTech's trust account and is the first cannabis software company listed on a major U.S. exchange.

Akerna consolidates cannabis technology companies to connect data points in the global cannabis supply chain. In doing so, Akerna creates one of the world's most transparent and accountable consumer packaged goods supply chain with global scale. We believe connected data and information will modernize and propel the cannabis industry increasing the power of businesses, governments, patients and consumers to make smart decisions.

The cornerstone service offerings is MJ Freeway, the world's largest, global cannabis software company that invented seed-to-sale tracking and developed the industry's first cannabis ERP. Established in 2010, MJ Freeway has to date tracked more than $18 billion in legal cannabis sales.

Founded in 2010 by technologists creating tech specifically for cannabis businesses, MJ Freeway's tracking software includes inventory control and grow management applications to streamline workflow and increase efficiency. MJ Freeway's Leaf Data Systems software solution enables governments to track cannabis plants from seed-to-sale and ensure patient, public, and product safety. MJ Freeway also offers a complete suite of professional consulting services for cannabis businesses. For more information, visit mjfreeway.com.

Source: www.akerna.com

Cannabis Is Not Their Main Business

PerkinElmer, Inc. (NYSE: PKI)

(Founded 1937; headquartered in Waltham, Massachusetts)

PerkinElmer is placed in the Life Sciences Tools & Services industry and has recently made a big move into the cannabis testing space. Cannabis is still a small part of the overall company's business. PerkinElmer is offering complete cannabis analysis solutions, including pesticide testing, potency and moisture qualification, contamination testing and prevention, and other areas of chemical analysis. Their cannabis-related business lines are growing quickly.

Corporate Description

PerkinElmer is a $2.9 billion global company committed to innovating for a healthier world. We create the instruments, tests and software used by scientists, researchers and clinicians to address the most critical challenges across science and healthcare.

We strategically partner with customers to enable earlier, more accurate insights, supported by deep market knowledge and technical expertise. Our dedicated team of about 13,000 employees is passionate about helping them work to create healthier families, improve the quality of life and sustain the wellbeing of people worldwide.

Through our comprehensive portfolio, we serve four market segments to help customers:

DIAGNOSTICS

Test expectant mothers for pregnancy-related health risks and fetal abnormalities

Screen newborn babies for genetic mutations that are associated with life-threatening disorders

Accelerate detection of rare diseases, autoimmune disorders, allergies and infectious diseases

LIFE SCIENCES

Advance innovations in cancer cells, infectious microorganisms and neurological pathways

Validate chemical compounds, molecular data and biomarker insights to uncover drug candidates

Develop more effective medicines and biotherapeutics, bringing treatments to market faster

FOOD

Maintain safety and quality of food/beverage products by detecting fraudulent ingredients or toxins

Analyze cannabis and hemp for unsafe pesticide levels, harmful residues and product impurities

Boost crop yield and enhance plant/grain quality to maximize productivity in sub-optimal conditions

APPLIED MARKETS

Ensure the air we breathe and water we drink are free of dangerous pollutants and contaminants

Detect and quantify concentrations of lead, heavy metals and other toxic elements in soil and water

Optimize performance and assure quality of industrial products (gas, biofuels lubricants, petrochemicals, polymers)

Around the world today, more than 2 million scientists are using PerkinElmer's laboratory software to store and analyze research data and collaborate on experiments. PerkinElmer technologies have contributed to the development of 22 novel therapeutic drugs.

Source: `perkinelmer.com/corporate/company/about-us/`
`fact-sheet.html`

Thermo Fisher Scientific Inc. *(NYSE: TMO)*

(Founded 1956; headquartered in Waltham, Massachusetts)

Thermo Fisher Scientific is a very large multinational healthcare company and like PerkinElmer, is officially described as being in the Life Sciences Tools & Services industry. Their market cap is more than $130 billion as of early 2020. Thermo Fisher offers analytical instruments, laboratory equipment, software, consumables, reagents, instrument systems, chemicals, supplies, and services worldwide. They have even been in the front lines of producing COVID-19 testing kits in 2020.

In the cannabis space, the company offers end-to-end solutions to comply with Health Canada cannabis testing standards. Company testing includes microbial contaminants and disintegration, THC and CBD content, moisture content, and nutritional information.

Additionally, Thermo Fisher has partnered with leading Canadian extraction firm Valens GroWorks in a multi-area research collaboration. Valens will utilize Thermo Fisher's instruments and materials in their study of cannabis.

Corporate Description

Thermo Fisher Scientific Inc. is the world leader in serving science, with annual revenue exceeding $25 billion. Our Mission is to enable our customers to make the world healthier, cleaner and safer. Whether our customers are accelerating life sciences research, solving complex analytical challenges, improving patient diagnostics and therapies or increasing productivity in their laboratories, we are here to support them. Our global team of more than 75,000 colleagues delivers an unrivaled combination of innovative technologies, purchasing convenience and pharmaceutical services through our industry-leading brands, including Thermo Scientific, Applied Biosystems, Invitrogen, Fisher Scientific, Unity Lab Services and Patheon.

Source: `corporate.thermofisher.com/en/about-us`

The Scotts Miracle-Gro Company (NYSE: SMG)

(Founded 1868; headquartered in Marysville, Ohio)

Scotts is another that many people now like to consider a cannabis company, but cannabis remains a comparatively small part of what it does. The Scotts Miracle-Gro Company is worth more than $7 billion. The company's main focus remains the manufacture and sale of consumer lawn and garden products around the world. But, Scotts has made a big commitment to the cannabis space with multiple hydroponic company acquisitions. Hawthorne Gardening is a wholly owned subsidiary that provides nutrients, lighting and other materials used for indoor and hydroponic growing.

Scotts' total annual sales exceed $3 billion per year. Hawthorne's are only around $200 million of that but growing like a weed.

Corporate Description

With approximately $3.2 billion in sales, the Company is one of the world's largest marketers of branded consumer products for lawn and garden care. The Company's brands are among the most

*recognized in the industry. The Company's Scotts®, Miracle-Gro®
and Ortho® brands are market-leading in their categories. The
Company's wholly-owned subsidiary, The Hawthorne Gardening
Company, is a leading provider of nutrients, lighting and other
materials used in the indoor and hydroponic growing segment.*

*Not many companies have roots as deep as ours. We've evolved
from a family general store to North America's leader in lawn and
garden as well as hydroponic growing products. We're headquartered in Marysville, Ohio, only five miles from where our company
was founded more than 150 years ago.*

*Our 5,800 associates form the heart and soul of our company,
making our vision a reality by delivering products and solutions that
help you create beautiful gardens, vibrant plants and landscapes
that thrive. Our legacy is rooted in trust, innovation and doing the
right thing—for today's gardeners and growers and the ones who
come tomorrow.*

Source: scottsmiraclegro.com/who-we-are

Chapter 15
Mergers and Acquisitions

"I'm into ... murders and executions, mostly."
– Patrick Bateman, *American Psycho*

Within the cannabis industry in both Canada and the United States, we have witnessed a rather constant stream of mergers and acquisitions. Generally larger and better funded publicly traded operators have acquired smaller licensed operators as a method to expand into markets where they didn't already have a presence, or as a way to grab additional market share away from competitors while adding to their overall size and revenue. An existing license is valuable. North America's cannabis industry currently has too many small, independent license holders. Some are privately held. Some are small, publicly traded penny stocks. With so many in existence, it is truly impossible to identify the best acquisition targets versus those that will simply be squeezed out of business. Many more will fail without value than be acquired.

After additional moves on cannabis legislation in the United States, the market could open up for significant merger and acquisition activity. If you are thinking that major food, retail, alcohol, and tobacco companies are soon going to take over and dominate the cannabis business, I believe you will be disappointed. With true US cannabis legalization still elusive, big non-cannabis companies cannot yet invest in US operators. Even as it relates to Canada's licensed producers, big corporations still want to keep their involvement in marijuana somewhat at arm's length, as a separate entity. While large corporations are looking hard at the cannabis industry, various forms of partnership, joint venture, or licensing agreements now seem more likely than any complete buy-outs. Large direct investment transactions for Big Pharma and major CPG (consumer packaged goods) companies similar to the deals of Altria and Constellation Brands seem very unlikely. Regardless of the odds for additional major acquisitions, a very important point to remember is that an investor should want to own the acquiree, not the acquirer. Altria and Constellation Brands' stock prices did not go up with the Cronos and Canopy Growth agreements. To date, Altria and Constellation have lost huge amounts of money on those deals. On the other hand, the acquiree – the firm getting acquired or partially acquired – should realize a nice boost in its stock price.

As a portfolio manager looking for real cannabis investments, I seek companies whose primary business is focused on cannabis – marijuana, hemp, CBD, or pharmaceuticals related to cannabinoids. Companies like Altria and Constellation Brands are now related to the cannabis business but are not really cannabis companies. While I applaud their vision, Altria is a tobacco company that sees cigarette sales continuing to dwindle, and wisely does not want to miss out on the cannabis boom. Constellation Brands was an aggressive early adopter in the cannabis space but remains primarily a well-diversified alcohol company. Constellation had the foresight to grab cannabis market share rather than just risk decreasing alcohol sales with increasing marijuana legalization. Numerous multi-billion-dollar corporations are dipping into the cannabis world. It remains to be seen just how integrated cannabis may become in the larger consumer packaged goods universe.

Constellation Brands, Inc. (NYSE: STZ)

(Founded 1945; headquartered in Victor, New York; approximate 2020 market capitalization $27 billion)

The alcohol company Constellation Brands became a consumer packaged goods first mover by purchasing into the cannabis business in October 2017. It acquired a 9.9% stake in Canadian LP Canopy Growth for $190 million. At the time, the move was widely applauded as it gained a foothold in the recreational marijuana market with Canada's leading cannabis company. While excitement was still high, Constellation increased its position in Canopy to 38% with an additional $4 billion investment in 2018. A bold move, but before the bottom fell out of cannabis stock prices in 2019.

Constellation has worked aggressively to cut costs and aid Canopy's probability profile. It remains to be seen if Constellation turns out to be a wise first mover in the long run – or that they vastly overpaid for their foothold in the cannabis space.

Altria Group, Inc. (NYSE: MO)

(Founded 1822; headquartered in Richmond, Virginia; approximate 2020 market capitalization $65 billion)

If Constellation Brands was a packaged goods first mover, Altria was a solid second. In December of 2018 the tobacco giant Altria Group announced plans to invest $1.8 billion for a 45% stake in Canadian LP Cronos. While Cronos Group had a nice resume among the Canadian licensed producers, its market share of Canadian cannabis sales has been sad. As mentioned in an earlier chapter, Altria and Cronos have been somewhat inactive to date toward marketing, branding, and sales. Altria may be in wait-and-see mode. Compared to Altria's primary business lines, Cronos is a small piece of the puzzle.

Imperial Brands PLC ADR (US OTC: IMBBY)

(Founded 1901; headquartered in Bristol, United Kingdom; approximate 2020 market capitalization $19 billion)

British tobacco giant Imperial Brands (owner of Kool and Winston cigarette brands among others) technically moved into cannabis before tobacco competitor Altria, but it did so without a massive investment like that of Altria and without gaining direct ownership. In mid-2018, Imperial announced that it had joined with seed investment firm Casa Verde (backed by Snoop Dogg!) to invest in British medical marijuana research firm Oxford Cannabinoid Technologies.

Anheuser-Busch InBev SA (NYSE: BUD)

(Founded 1366; headquartered in Leuven, Belgium; approximate 2020 market capitalization $71 billion)

It seems crazy that the Anheuser-Busch we all knew as headquartered in St. Louis, Missouri, is now Anheuser-Busch InBev of Belgium and founded way back in 1366. Like some other alcohol and tobacco companies acting on cannabis excitement in 2018, Anheuser-Busch announced that it would form a joint venture with Canadian LP Tilray for $50 million each for cannabis-infused beverages of both the THC and CBD variety. Tilray would work with Anheuser-Busch InBev subsidiary Labatt Brewing initially with drinks confined to the Canadian market. Although cannabis beverages have yet to take off in a major way, the joint venture route seems much smarter than Constellation Brands large equity investments.

Molson Coors Beverage Company (NYSE: TAP)

(Founded 1873; headquartered in Denver, Colorado; approximate 2020 market capitalization $7 billion)

Following the lead of other alcohol and tobacco companies, beer giant Molson Coors announced in October of 2019 that it had agreed to a partnership with Canada's cannabis LP HEXO to create cannabis-infused beverages. The partnership's Truss Beverage Company initially planned to launch six nonalcoholic, cannabis beverage brands in Canada. The first would be Flow Glow, a cannabis-infused spring water. Molson has stated that it believes the Canadian cannabis beverage market could reach $3 billion in value.

Earlier in the year, Molson had signaled that it had eyeballs on the cannabis space and fears of legal marijuana's impact of the alcohol industry. In a 2019 regulatory filing with the US Securities and Exchange Commission, Molson stated: "Although the ultimate impact is currently unknown, the emergence of legal cannabis in certain US states and Canada may result in a shift of discretionary income away from our products or a change in consumer preferences away from beer." Interesting.

Chapter 16
Don't Get Burned

"The investor's chief problem – and even his worst enemy – is likely to be himself."

– Benjamin Graham

The choice of investing in individual stocks or using managed portfolios and exchange traded funds (ETFs) is up to each investor, or investment team, or advisor. I am biased, but I believe in the use of ETFs as the most efficient trading vehicle. As a portfolio manager, I can do things at an institutional level that individual investors simply cannot, such as the lending of portfolio securities to create quarterly fund income payments or ETF basket trades to minimize capital gains taxes. If an investor does want to choose their own stocks, I would invite them to follow what I do as a cannabis fund portfolio manager. There is nothing to hide. An exchange-traded fund's website lists complete portfolio holdings on a daily basis.

I am also biased toward investing in public, exchange-listed stocks – with the regulatory oversight and reporting that goes along with public stocks. It seems that almost everyone has heard about a friend of a relative, or neighbor, or co-worker who is involved in some type of cannabis opportunity. I would stay away from private deals and local investments. Like any entrepreneurial start-up business, most will not make it. Only a few will lead to great success stories. Many entrepreneurs are great idea people, but lousy businesspeople. Cannabis investing already has plenty of upside and plenty of risk. Stick to larger publicly traded stocks and ETFs.

For legal and compliance reasons, I am not going to describe individual cannabis related ETFs by name, but I will tell you what I like and do not like.

Actively Managed

I believe in active portfolio management. A fund's portfolio manager should use information available to make decisions on the stocks to own, which to avoid, and when to trade. On the other hand, cannabis-focused exchange-traded funds that are based on an index seem rather stupid to me. In a very rapidly changing and volatile area such as cannabis, I would never want to invest by blindly following an index. An index fund is often weighted just by the size (market cap) of the companies they invest in. There is no portfolio manager making the investment decisions within the fund. With a large, diversified US index like the S&P 500, index investing makes perfect sense. The best performing companies often become the index's largest companies and largest portfolio weightings. Widely diversified, large company index funds with low fees can often outperform. You get stocks like Apple and Amazon in the largest percentage. With a relatively new industry like cannabis? The largest market cap companies could very well be among the worst investments.

Exchange-traded funds are transparent. That means they are required to post their portfolio holdings for public view before each trading day. In considering an ETF, look at the fund's top holdings. With an index-based fund in the cannabis space, you will almost always see top holdings in what I call "the usual suspects" of large Canadian LPs – Canopy, Cronos, Aurora, Tilray. I think you can do better.

Don't follow an index. Active portfolio management and active cannabis stock selection, while still diversified, is the way to go.

Pure Cannabis

Whether an investor is choosing their own stocks or using exchange-traded funds, cannabis investments should only make up a predetermined percentage of an overall portfolio. I can't tell you what that percentage should be. It depends on an investor's individual situation and risk tolerance. Cannabis investments are very volatile. Cannabis investments are high risk or speculative in nature. Any investment portfolio, whether individual or institutional, should be soundly diversified with investments that are less volatile than cannabis stocks.

I think a fund described as a cannabis fund should be just that – a cannabis fund. If an investor is properly diversified elsewhere, there should be no need for non-cannabis stocks within their cannabis fund. Companies like Altria, Constellation Brands, Scotts Miracle-Gro, Abbvie, and others could be good investments in general, but don't kid yourself thinking that they are cannabis companies. They are not. Their primary focus is elsewhere. If an investment portfolio already holds an S&P 500 index fund or other diversified large company fund, the portfolio already holds stocks like Altria, Constellation Brands, Scotts Miracle-Gro, and Abbvie. I am a big believer in having investors know and understand what they invest in. I manage two funds for pure cannabis investments. I manage another fund for indirect, cannabis-related investments combined with alcohol and tobacco "vice" investments.

While the funds that I manage are of good size and trade very efficiently in my opinion, there are other very small cannabis-related ETFs in existence. Don't be confused and think that because a fund is small or lightly traded that it is illiquid. Any exchange-traded fund's liquidity is based on the fund's underlying holdings. That means that most ETFs that hold exchange-listed stocks are perfectly liquid. But to be blunt, a tiny fund might trade like crap. A tiny fund could trade with big spreads between its bid and ask price (sell and buy price). A fund could go through portions of the day without trading at all, causing its price to look much different than its real value. A lightly traded fund could close the day without a recent trade, creating a significant premium or discount compared to its end-of-day real value (its NAV or net asset value price). Some people might call it inefficient trading. A nicer term to use may be to say that some ETFs do not always trade smoothly.

Trade Orders

The most common types of orders are market orders, limit orders, and stop-loss orders.

A market order is an order to buy or sell a security immediately. This type of order guarantees that the order will be executed, but does not guarantee the execution price. A market order generally will execute at or near the current bid (for a sell order) or ask (for a buy order) price. However, it is important for investors to remember that the last-traded price is not necessarily the price at which a market order will be executed.

A limit order is an order to buy or sell a security at a specific price or better. A buy limit order can only be executed at the limit price or lower, and a sell limit order can only be executed at the limit price or higher. Example: An investor wants to purchase shares of ABC stock for no more than $10. The investor could submit a limit order for this amount and this order will only execute if the price of ABC stock is $10 or lower.

A stop order, also referred to as a stop-loss order, is an order to buy or sell a stock once the price of the stock reaches the specified price, known as the stop price. When the stop price is reached, a stop order becomes a market order.

A buy stop order is entered at a stop price above the current market price. Investors generally use a buy stop order to limit a loss or protect a profit on a stock that they have sold short. *A sell stop order* is entered at a stop price below the current market price. Investors generally use a sell stop order to limit a loss or protect a profit on a stock they own.

Source: investor.gov

Use Limit Orders

In making a trade for an ETF, use limit orders. Do not place a market order. With a market order, you are subject to the ETF's (or stock's) prevailing bid / ask price at any point in time and may simply pay too much or receive too little. Investors don't have to accept that. By simply placing a limit order between the posted bid / ask price, an investor should be able to get a good execution price on a trade. Better yet, before anyone places a trade at a brokerage firm they should call the fund company and discuss how to best place the order. A fund company representative should be able to easily quote the fund's value at any time of the trading day and help with where to set a limit price. If placing a relatively large buy or sell order for a fund, always call first. A fund company like mine can communicate with institutional trade desks and market making firms to help assure a smooth trade and an accurate price.

ETF Primer

An exchange-traded fund (ETF) is a pooled investment fund whose shares are traded on an exchange. ETFs are bought and sold by a broker. In the United States, ETFs can be found on the NYSE, or the NASDAQ.

ETF History

ETFs were first introduced in the early 1990s in the United States and Canada and over the ensuing years the number of ETFs traded worldwide and the value of their assets under management have increased substantially.

ETFs are now a global product tracking the performance of broad-based equity indices, sector-specific indexes and

(continued)

(*continued*)

other asset classes such as fixed income, metals, and commodities.

Actively managed ETFs are new investment vehicles that will allow investors to participate in an actively managed portfolio strategy that could range from tactical to traditional asset allocation and from sophisticated currency strategies to emerging markets.

Active ETF basics:

- An actively managed ETF is an exchange-trade fund that is managed by a single or team of fund managers.
- An actively managed ETF uses a professional portfolio manager who selects the securities to be included based on the investment strategy.

Actively managed ETF features:

- Ability to react to changing markets
- Discretionary money management
- Liquidity
- Transparency
- Investment strategies that seek to outperform index benchmarks

Historically, actively managed investment strategies have been most easily accessible through mutual funds. Today, investors can utilize the same types of investment strategies and professional money management with all of the features that ETFs provide, including:

- Liquidity
- Transparency
- Tax efficiency

The combination of active management and the ETF features provide investors an innovative new solution to manage their investment strategy to achieve their investment goals.

ETFS Versus Mutual Funds Comparison

The table below summarizes the key structure of actively managed ETFs versus traditional ETFs and mutual funds.

Feature	Active ETF	Index ETF	Mutual Fund
Marginable	YES	YES	NO
Shortable	YES	YES	NO
Tax Efficient*	YES	YES	MAYBE
Trades Intraday	YES	YES	NO
Ability to Produce Alpha	YES	NO	MAYBE
Passive Management	NO	YES	MAYBE

*ETFs are, however, subject to commission costs each time you buy or sell.

ETF FAQs

- How can I buy or sell ETFs?

  ETFs are listed with ticker symbols in the same way as individual stocks. They can be bought or sold throughout the day by a full service or discount broker. A brokerage commission to buy or sell will usually apply.
- How long have ETFs been trading and available for investors to purchase?

(continued)

(continued)

    ETFs were first introduced in the early 1990s in the United States and Canada and over the ensuing years the number of ETFs traded worldwide and the value of their assets under management have increased substantially. ETFs are now a global product category tracking the performance of broad-based equity indexes, sector specific equity indexes and are used to invest in other asset classes such as fixed income, currencies and commodities. More recently, active managers have been using ETFs as a platform to reach investors nationally.

- How many ETFs are currently trading?

    There are currently more than 1,500 individual ETFs available to purchase and trade on US exchanges.

- How is an ETF different from a mutual fund?

    ETFs offer investors intraday liquidity and can be bought and sold with a brokerage account. Mutual funds are priced at the end of the day and cannot be bought or sold during regular trading hours. Also, ETFs are traded on a stock exchange, whereas mutual funds are bought and sold directly with the fund company or through a mutual fund trading platform.

- Can ETFs be sold short?

    Yes. One of the potential advantages of ETFs is that they trade on an exchange similar to equities and if available may be sold short.

Source: advisorshares.com/education

Appendix I
Portfolio Manager Dan Ahrens' Cannabis Exchange-traded Fund Holdings on June 30, 2020

Symbol	Company	Portfolio Weight (%)
IIPR	Innovative Industrial Properties	9.41
VFF	Village Farms International	9.17
GWPH	GW Pharmaceuticals – ADR	8.06
GTBIF	Green Thumb Industries Swap	6.64
CURLF	Curaleaf Holdings Inc. Swap	6.26
TCNNF	Trulieve Cannabis Swap	6.06
ARNA	Arena Pharmaceuticals Inc.	5.68
APHA	Aphria Inc.	5.38
GRWG	Growgeneration Corp.	4.94
OGI	Organigram Holdings Inc.	4.20
VLNS	Valens Groworks Corp.	4.11

Symbol	Company	Portfolio Weight (%)
CGC	Canopy Growth Corporation	3.56
CRBP	Corbus Pharmaceuticals Holdings	3.52
CGC	Canopy Growth Corporation	3.51
ZYNE	Zynerba Pharmaceuticals Inc.	2.83
NEPT	Neptune Wellness Solutions	2.64
GNLN	Greenlane Holdings Inc.	2.54
CWEB	Charlottes Web Holdings Inc.	2.18
ALEF	Aleafia Health Inc.	2.10
RIV	Canopy Rivers Inc.	1.98
YCBD	CBDMD Inc.	1.85
CRLBF	Cresco Labs Inc. Swap	0.97
CRDL	Cardiol Therapeutics	0.93
LABS	Medipharm Labs Corp	0.87
KHRN	Khiron Life Sciences Corp.	0.48
WMD	WeedMD Inc.	0.47
EMH	Emerald Health Therapeutics	0.37
FIRE	The Supreme Cannabis Company	0.34
TGOD	Green Organic Dutchman Holdings	0.33
ACB	Aurora Cannabis Inc.	0.33
NTEC	Intec Pharma Ltd.	0.28
HEXO	HEXO Corp.	0.26
TLRY	Tilray Inc. – Class 2 Common	0.19
ITHUF	Ianthus Capital Holdings Swap	0.18
	Net Cash	0.96

Source: AdvisorShares.

Appendix II

Portfolio Manager Dan Ahrens' US Cannabis Exchange-traded Fund Planned Holdings in August 2020

Symbol	Company	Portfolio Weight (%)
GTBIF	Green Thumb Industries Swap	8.50
CURLF	Curaleaf Holdings Inc. Swap	8.50
TCNNF	Trulieve Cannabis Swap	8.50
IIPR	Innovative Industrial Properties	8.00
GRWG	Growgeneration Corp.	6.00
CCHWF	Columbia Care Inc. Swap	5.00
CRLBF	Cresco Labs Inc. Swap	5.00

Symbol	Company	Portfolio Weight (%)
ARNA	Arena Pharmaceuticals Inc.	4.50
YCBD	CBDMD Inc.	4.50
AYRSF	AYR Strategies Inc. Swap	4.50
TRSSF	Terrascend Corp. Swap	4.00
CWEB	Charlottes Web Holdings Inc.	4.00
CRBP	Corbus Pharmaceuticals	3.50
PKI	PerkinElmer Inc.	3.00
GNLN	Greenlane Holdings Inc.	3.00
ZYNE	Zynerba Pharmaceuticals Inc.	3.00
PLNHF	Planet 13 Holdings Swap	2.50
ACRGF	Acreage Holdings Inc. Swap	2.00
HRVSF	Harvest Health & Rec Swap	2.00
SSPK	Silver Spike Acquisition Corp.	2.00
JUSHF	Jushi Holdings Inc. Swap	2.00
KERN	Akerna Corp.	2.00
PW	Power REIT	1.50
NBEV	New Age Beverages Corp.	1.50
	Net Cash	1.00

Source: AdvisorShares.

Appendix III

Constituents of the North American Marijuana Index as of June 30, 2020

The North American Marijuana Index tracks the leading cannabis stocks operating in the United States and Canada. Constituents must have a business strategy focused on the marijuana or hemp industry and are required to meet our minimum trading criteria. The Index is equal-weighted and rebalanced quarterly.

Symbol	Company
CGC	Canopy Growth Corporation
GWPH	GW Pharmaceuticals Plc
CURLF	Curaleaf Holdings Inc.
CRON	Cronos Group Inc.
IIPR	Innovative Industrial Properties Inc.
GTBIF	Green Thumb Industries Inc.
TCNNF	Trulieve Cannabis Corp.
ACB	Aurora Cannabis Inc.
APHA	Aphria Inc.
TLRY	Tilray Inc.
CRLBF	Cresco Labs Inc.
HEXO	HEXO Corp.

Symbol	Company
CWBHF	Charlotte's Web Holdings Inc.
NEPT	Neptune Wellness Solutions Inc.
OGI	Organigram Holdings Inc.
VLNS:CA	Valens GroWorks Corp.
FFNTF	4Front Ventures Corp.
GRWG	GrowGeneration Corp.
ACRGF	Acreage Holdings
PLNHF	Planet 13 Holdings Inc.
XLY:CA	Auxly Cannabis Group Inc.
RIV:CA	Canopy Rivers Inc.
GNLN	Greenlane Holdings Inc.
LABS:CA	MediPharm Labs Corp.
TRSSF	TerrAscend Corp
AYRSF	AYR Strategies Inc.
TLLTF	TILT Holdings Inc.
LHSIF	Liberty Health Sciences
FAF:CA	Fire & Flower Holdings Corp.
HRVSF	Harvest Health & Recreation Inc.
YCBD	cbdMD Inc.
SNDL	Sundial Growers Inc.
FIRE:CA	The Supreme Cannabis Company Inc.
KSHB	KushCo Holdings Inc.
MMNFF	MedMen Enterprises Inc.
CNTMF	Cansortium Inc.
VREOF	Vireo Health International Inc.
CVSI	CV Sciences Inc.
ZENA:CA	Zenabis Global Inc.
CNTTQ	CannTrust Holdings Inc.
DN:CA	Delta 9 Cannabis Inc.
MRMD	MariMed Inc.
ITHUF	iAnthus Capital Holdings Inc.
META:CA	Meta Growth Corp.
TRTC	Terra Tech Corp.
INDXF	Indus Holdings Inc.
HBOR:CNX	Harborside Inc.
GGBXF	Green Growth Brands Inc.
CXXIF	C21 Investments Inc.

Source: https://marijuanaindex.com

About the Author

Dan Ahrens is the portfolio manager of AdvisorShares Pure Cannabis ETF (NYSE: YOLO) and AdvisorShares Pure US Cannabis ETF (NYSE: MSOS). He acts as chief operating officer of AdvisorShares Investments, LLC. Dan carries well over two decades of experience in the financial services industry serving in a variety of senior-level capacities, including portfolio management, sales management, finance, operations, and compliance. Among many investment funds he has brought to market or managed, he launched the Vice Fund (VICEX) in 2002 and served as its original portfolio manager. Dan is the author of *Investing in Vice* (St. Martin's Press, 2004) and has appeared prominently across financial media outlets and major national and trade publications.

Visit his firm's website at www.advisorshares.com.

This is not an offer to buy any AdvisorShares funds.

Index

A

Abacus Health Products Inc., 120

AbbVie Inc., 156

acquisitions. *See* mergers and acquisitions

Acreage Holdings, Inc., 119, 120, 132–134

actively managed portfolios, 176

Adastra Labs Holding Ltd., 104

Affinor Growers Inc., 104

AgraFlora Organics International, 104

Agrios Global Holdings Ltd., 120

Ahrens, Dan, 183–186

Akerna Corp., 163–164

Alabama, 78, 91

Alaska, 78

alcohol industry
  cannabis and, 22
  characteristics of, 9–10
  compared to cannabis industry, 10–11
  history of, 3–12

Aleafia Health Inc., 100, 102

Alliance Growers Corp., 104

Almirall SA, 150

Altria Group, Inc., 40–41, 67, 70, 98, 112, 115, 171

Amazon, 30

AMP German Cannabis Group Inc., 104

Anheuser-Busch InBev SA, 11, 112, 172

Anslinger, Harry, 14–15, 16

Aphria Inc., 100, 101, 102, 109–110

Apple, 31–32

Arena Pharmaceuticals, Inc., 155–156

Argentina, medical use of cannabis in, 96

Arizona, 78, 85

Arkansas, 78, 89

Ascent Industries Corp., 120

Asia, cannabis use in, 96

Asia Green Biotechnology Corp., 104

ATF (Bureau of Alcohol, Tobacco, Firearms and Explosives), 62

Aurora Cannabis Inc., 100, 101, 102, 113–115

Australis Capital Inc., 120

Avicanna Inc., 102

Ayr Strategies Inc., 119, 120

B

Bank Secrecy Act (BSA) (1970), 18

banking
　Canadian LPs and, 66–67
　Federal legislation and, 54–55
　in United States, 70

barriers to entry, as an alcohol industry characteristic, 9–10

Bayer HealthCare AG, 150

beauty industry, cannabis and, 23

Beleave Inc., 104

Benchmark Botanics Inc., 104

BevCanna Enterprises Inc., 104

Bhang Inc., 120

Bierman, Adam, 132

Big Tobacco, 22

Biome Grow Inc., 104

biotech stocks, 149–157

black-market cannabis sales, 27, 71

Blockbuster, 32–33

Blueberries Medical Corp., 105

Blumenauer, Earl, 57, 58

Body and Mind Inc., 120

Bonaparte, Napoleon, 14

Bureau of Alcohol, Tobacco, Firearms and Explosives (ATF), 62

buy stop order, 178

C

C21 Investments Inc., 120

California, 45–46, 71–72, 78, 80–81

Calyx Ventures Inc., 103

Canada. See also Canada LPs
　Cannabis 2.0, 68–69
　Cannabis Act (2018), 45
　cannabis dispensaries in, 37
　cannabis stocks in, 42
　enterprise value in, 66
　industry pros and cons, 66
　legalization of cannabis in, 36–37, 65, 95
　United States compared with, 65–74

Canada House Wellness Group Inc., 105

Canada LPs
  about, 65–67, 74, 97–98
  investing, 99–106
  recommended, 107–116
CanadaBis Capital Inc., 103
Canadian Securities Exchange
  (CSE)
  about, 104–106
  US-based cannabis stocks on,
    120–122
  US-based MSOs on, 69–70
CanaFarma Hemp Products
  Corp., 105
cannabichromene (CBC), 25
cannabidiol (CBD), 23, 24–25,
  39–40
Cannabidiol and Marijuana
  Research Expansion Act, 57
cannabigerol (CBG), 25
cannabinol (CBN), 25
cannabis. *See also specific topics*
  about, 24–25
  industries of, 21–26
  legalization of, 10–11, 13,
    36–37, 45–63, 65, 73–74,
    95–96
  prohibition of, 13–14, 16
Cannabis 2.0, 68–69
Cannabis Act (2018), 45
cannabis beverages, 11–12
cannabis dispensaries, 37, 41–42
cannabis funds, 177–178
Cannabis Growth Opportunity
  Corp., 105
cannabis industry, compared to
  alcohol industry, 10–11

cannabis market
  growth of, 26–27
  growth of in US, 75–76
Cannabis One Holdings Inc.,
  120
cannabis stocks
  during 2019, 36–37
  during 2020, 41
  in Canada, 42
  cannabidiol (CBD), 39–40
  financial concerns, 40–41
  future of, 41–42
  short selling, 37–38
  in the US, 42–43
  vaping, 39
  volatility and, 33–43
cannabis tourism industry, 23
Cannabix Technologies Inc.,
  105
CannAmerica Brands Corp.,
  120
CannaOne Technologies Inc.,
  105
Cannara Biotech Inc., 105
Canna-V-Cell Sciences Inc., 105
Canntab Therapeutics Ltd., 105
CannTrust Holdings Inc., 102
Canopy Growth Corporation,
  40–41, 67, 98, 100, 101, 102,
  110–112, 114, 115, 133–134
Cansortium Inc., 120
Captiva Verde Land Corp., 105
Captor Capital Corp., 120
Cardiol Therapeutics Inc., 102,
  154–155
CardiolRxTM, 154–155

CARERS Act, 59
Catalent, Inc., 157
CB2 Insights Inc., 105
CBC (cannabichromene), 25
CBD (cannabidiol), 23, 24–25, 39–40
CBD Global Sciences Inc., 120
CBD-focused stocks
  about, 141–142
  honorable mention, 146–147
  recommended best, 143–146
cbdMD, Inc., 144–146
CBG (cannabigerol), 25
CBN (cannabinol), 25
Center for Research in Security Prices (CRSP), 3
Charlotte's Web Holdings, Inc., 143–144
Chemesis International Inc., 120
Chemistree Technology Inc., 120
Chile, medical use of cannabis in, 96
Choom Holdings Inc., 105
Citation Growth Corp., 120
City View Green Holdings Inc., 105
Clarifying Law Around Insurance of Marijuana Act (2019), 54–55
Clean Slate Act of 2019, 59
CLS Holdings USA, Inc., 120
CNSX Markets Inc., 104
CO_2 GRO Inc., 103
Cole Memo, 50–52

Colorado, 46, 72–73, 76–80, 78
Columbia, medical use of cannabis in, 96
Columbia Care Inc., 119, 120
Combatting Impaired Driving Act of 2019, 59
Community Reinvestment Fund, 61
competition, in alcohol industry, 10
concentrates, 135–138
concentration, as an alcohol industry characteristic, 9–10
Connecticut, 78, 87
Constellation Brands, Inc., 11, 40–41, 67, 70, 98, 110–111, 112, 171
construction industry, cannabis and, 23
Controlled Substance Act (CSA) (1970), 17, 60, 61
Corbus Pharmaceuticals Holdings, Inc., 152
CordovaCann Corp., 105
cotton gin, 16
COVID-19, 9, 41–42, 43, 49–50, 68, 86, 87, 89, 90, 91, 133, 145, 166
Cresco Labs Inc., 119, 120, 129–130
Croatia, medical use of cannabis in, 96
Cronos Group Inc., 40–41, 67, 98, 100, 101, 102, 114, 115–116, 171

CRSP (Center for Research in Security Prices), 3
CSE (Canadian Securities Exchange). *See* Canadian Securities Exchange (CSE)
Cuomo, Andrew, 49, 86
Curaleaf Holdings, Inc., 118, 120, 126–127
CV Sciences, Inc., 146–147

D
DEA (Drug Enforcement Agency), 17, 18
Delaware, 78, 87
Delta 9 Cannabis Inc., 102
delta-9-tetrahydrocanabinol (THC), 23, 24
demographics, legalization support and, 46–48
Department of Health and Human Services, 61
Department of Housing and Urban Development, 61
Department of Justice, 61
Department of Labor, 61
Department of Veterans Affairs Policy for Medicinal Cannabis Use Act of 2019, 59
dilution, stock, 40
dispensaries, 37, 41–42
District of Columbia, 78
Dixie Brands Inc., 120
Dravet syndrome, 143, 150, 151
Drug Enforcement Agency (DEA), 17, 18
drugs (medical)
classification of, 17
development of modern, 16
Du Pont family, 14
DuPont chemical company, 14, 15, 16

E
Eastwest Bioscience Inc., 103
e-commerce industry, cannabis and, 23
Eighteenth Amendment, to the Constitution, 1–2
EMA (European Medicines Agency), 151
Emerald Health Therapeutics, Inc., 103
Empower Clinics Inc., 120
Ending Federal Marijuana Prohibition Act of 2019, 59
endocannabinoids, 25–26
Ensuring Access to Counseling and Training for All Small Businesses Act of 2019, 59
Ensuring Safe Capital Access for All Small Business Act of 2019, 59
enterprise value, in Canada, 66
Epidiolex, 150, 151
ETFs (exchange-traded funds), 35, 176, 179–186
Eureka 93 Inc., 105
Eurolife Brands Inc., 105
European Medicines Agency (EMA), 151
Eve & Co. Inc., 103
Eviana Health Corp., 105

exchange-traded funds (ETFs),
    35, 176, 179–186
EXMceuticals Inc., 105
Expanding Cannabis Research
    and Information bill, 60
Experion Holdings Ltd., 103
extraction and concentrates,
    135–138

F
Fairness in Federal Drug
    Testing Under State Laws
    Act, 60
Farm Bill (2018), 52–53,
    141–142
FBN (Federal Bureau of
    Narcotics), 14–15
FDA (Food and Drug
    Administration), 18, 141–142
Federal Bureau of Narcotics
    (FBN), 14–15
Federal legislation
    Cannabidiol and Marijuana
        Research Expansion Act,
        57
    CARERS Act, 59
    Clarifying Law Around
        Insurance of Marijuana
        Act (2019), 54–55
    Clean Slate Act of 2019, 59
    Cole Memo, 50–52
    Combatting Impaired Driving
        Act of 2019, 59
    Department of Veterans
        Affairs Policy for Medicinal

Cannabis Use Act of 2019,
    59
Ending Federal Marijuana
    Prohibition Act of 2019, 59
Ensuring Access to
    Counseling and Training
    for All Small Businesses
    Act of 2019, 59
Ensuring Safe Capital Access
    for All Small Business Act
    of 2019, 59
Expanding Cannabis
    Research and Information
    bill, 60
Fairness in Federal Drug
    Testing Under State Laws
    Act, 60
Farm Bill (2018), 52–53,
    141–142
Homegrown Act of 2019, 60
Immigration and Nationality
    Act amendment, 58
Impaired Driving Study Act,
    60
LUMMA (Legitimate Use of
    Medicinal Marihuana Act),
    60
MAPLE Act, 60
Marijuana 1-to-3 Act of 2019,
    61
Marijuana Data Collection
    Act, 61
Marijuana Freedom and
    Opportunity Act, 56

Marijuana in Federally
     Assisted Housing Parity
     Act of 2019, 61
Marijuana Justice Act, 61
Marijuana Revenue and
     Regulation Act, 61
Medical Cannabis Research
     Act of 2019, 56–57
Medical Marijuana Research
     Act of 2019, 57
MORE Act (2019), 55–56
Next Step Act, 61
REFER Act of 2019, 61
Regulate Marijuana Like
     Alcohol Act, 61–62
Removing Marijuana from
     Deportable Offenses Act,
     62
Respect States' and Citizens'
     Rights Act of 2019, 62
Responsibly Addressing the
     Marijuana Policy Gap Act
     of 2019, 62
SAFE Act (2019), 53–54
Second Amendment
     Protection Act, 62
Second Chance for Students
     Act, 62
Sensible Business Tax Equity
     Act of 2019, 62
State Cannabis Commerce
     Act, 62
STATES Act, 55
Tribal Marijuana Sovereignty
     Act of 2019, 63

VA Medicinal Cannabis
     Research Act of 2019, 63
VA Survey of Cannabis Use
     Act, 63
Veterans Affairs bills, 62–63
Veterans Cannabis Use for
     Safe Healing Act, 63
Veteran's Equal Access Act,
     57–58
Veteran's Medical Marijuana
     Safe Harbor Act, 58
Feinstein, Dianne, 57
Figi, Charlotte, 143
financial concerns, for cannabis
     stocks, 40–41
FinCanna Capital Corp., 105
Florida, 78, 84–85
Flower One Holdings Inc., 120
Flowr Corporation, The, 103
Fluent, 112
Food and Drug Administration
     (FDA), 18, 141–142
48North Cannabis Corp., 103
4Front Ventures Corp., 120
French, Kenneth, 3
FSD Pharma Inc., 105
Future Farm Technologies Inc.,
     105

G
GABY Inc., 120
Gaia Grow Corp., 103, 105
Gardner, Cody, 55
Georgia (state), 78
Georgia (country), legalization
     of cannabis in, 95

Germany, medical use of
   cannabis in, 96
Geyser Brands Inc., 103
Gillibrand, Kristen, 56
Global Health Clinics Ltd., 105
Global Hemp Group Inc., 120
global use, of cannabis, 95–96
Golden Leaf Holdings Ltd., 121
Great Depression, 2–3
Greece, medical use of cannabis
   in, 96
Green Growth Brands Inc., 105
"green rush", 36
Green Thumb Industries Inc.,
   118, 121, 125–126
Greenlane Holdings, Inc.,
   161–162
GreenStar Biosciences Corp.,
   121
The Green Organic Dutchman,
   100, 102
GrowGeneration Corp.,
   160–161
Grown Rogue International
   Inc., 121
GTEC Holdings Ltd., 103
Guy, Geoffrey, 151
GW Pharmaceuticals plc,
   150–151

H
Harborside Inc., 121
Harris, Kamala, 56
Harvest Health & Recreation
   Inc., 119, 121, 130–131
Harvest One Cannabis Inc., 103

hash, smoking, 14
Hawaii, 78
Health Canada, 37
health industry, cannabis and,
   23
Hearst, William Randolph,
   14–15
Heineken, 11
hemp, uses for, 13–14, 15–16
Hemp for Health Inc., 105
hemp-focused stocks, 141–147
Heritage Cannabis Holdings
   Corp., 105
HEXO Corp., 100, 101, 102
Hi-Fi Hops, 11
High Tide Inc., 105
Hollister Biosciences Inc., 121
Homegrown Act of 2019, 60
Hoover, Herbert, 3
Humboldt, California, 72

I
iAnthus Capital Holdings Inc.,
   121
Icanic Brands Company Inc.,
   105
Idaho, 78, 90
Ignite International Brands,
   Ltd., 121
Illinois, 49, 78, 81–82
IM Cannabis Corp., 105
Immigration and Nationality
   Act amendment, 58
Impaired Driving Study Act, 60
Imperial Brands PLC ADR,
   172

income taxes, 2–3
Indiana, 78
INDIVA Ltd., 103
industries
    alcohol, 3–12, 22
    beauty, 23
    cannabis tourism, 23
    construction, 23
    e-commerce, 23
    health, 23
    non-alcoholic beverage, 22
    pet product, 23
    pharmaceutical, 23, 149–157
    real estate industry, 23
    statistics on, 4–5
    tobacco, 4, 15, 22, 23
    wellness, 23
infantile spasms, 150
InMed Pharmaceuticals Inc.,
    102
Inner Spirit Holdings Ltd., 105
Innovative Industrial
    Properties, Inc., 122–124,
    125
International Cannabrands
    Inc., 121
investing. *See also specific topics*
    in Canada LPs, 99–106
    choices for, 175–176
Invictus MD Strategies Corp.,
    103
Ionic Brands Corp., 121
Iowa, 78
Ipsen Biopharm Ltd., 150
Isracann Biosciences Inc., 105

J
James E. Wagner Cultivation
    Corp., 103
Jefferson, Thomas, 13–14
Jobs, Steve, 31
Jushi Holdings Inc., 121
"Just Say No" anti-drug
    campaign, 18

K
Kansas, 78
Kentucky, 78, 91
Khiron Life Sciences Corp., 103
Klein, David, 111
KushCo Holdings, Inc., 162–163

L
Lamont, Ned, 87
Leary, Timothy, 17
legalization
    in Canada, 65
    in Canada compared with
        United States, 73–74
    Federal legislation and, 50–63
    global, 95–96
    statistics on support for,
        45–50
legislation
    Cannabidiol and Marijuana
        Research Expansion Act,
        57
    CARERS Act, 59
    Clarifying Law Around
        Insurance of Marijuana
        Act (2019), 54–55
    Clean Slate Act of 2019, 59

legislation (*continued*)
Cole Memo, 50–52
Combatting Impaired Driving
Act of 2019, 59
Department of Veterans
Affairs Policy for Medicinal
Cannabis Use Act of 2019,
59
Ending Federal Marijuana
Prohibition Act of 2019, 59
Ensuring Access to
Counseling and Training
for All Small Businesses
Act of 2019, 59
Ensuring Safe Capital Access
for All Small Business Act
of 2019, 59
Expanding Cannabis
Research and Information
bill, 60
Fairness in Federal Drug
Testing Under State Laws
Act, 60
Farm Bill (2018), 52–53,
141–142
Homegrown Act of 2019, 60
Immigration and Nationality
Act amendment, 58
Impaired Driving Study Act,
60
LUMMA (Legitimate Use of
Medicinal Marihuana Act),
60
MAPLE Act, 60
Marijuana 1-to-3 Act of 2019,
61

Marijuana Data Collection
Act, 61
Marijuana Freedom and
Opportunity Act, 56
Marijuana in Federally
Assisted Housing Parity
Act of 2019, 61
Marijuana Justice Act, 61
Marijuana Revenue and
Regulation Act, 61
Medical Cannabis Research
Act of 2019, 56–57
Medical Marijuana Research
Act of 2019, 57
MORE Act (2019), 55–56
Next Step Act, 61
REFER Act of 2019, 61
Regulate Marijuana Like
Alcohol Act, 61–62
Removing Marijuana from
Deportable Offenses Act,
62
Respect States' and Citizens'
Rights Act of 2019, 62
Responsibly Addressing the
Marijuana Policy Gap Act
of 2019, 62
SAFE Act (2019), 53–54
Second Amendment
Protection Act, 62
Second Chance for Students
Act, 62
Sensible Business Tax Equity
Act of 2019, 62
State Cannabis Commerce
Act, 62

STATES Act, 55
states with pending new,
    86–91
states with potential new, 86
Tribal Marijuana Sovereignty
    Act of 2019, 63
VA Medicinal Cannabis
    Research Act of 2019, 63
VA Survey of Cannabis Use
    Act, 63
Veterans Affairs bills, 62–63
Veterans Cannabis Use for
    Safe Healing Act, 63
Veteran's Equal Access Act,
    57–58
Veteran's Medical Marijuana
    Safe Harbor Act, 58
Lennox-Gastaut syndrome, 150,
    151
Level Brands, Inc., 144
Leviathan Cannabis Group Inc.,
    105
Lexaria Bioscience Corp., 121
Liberty Health Sciences Inc.,
    121
Liberty Leaf Holdings Ltd., 105
licensed producers. *See* Canada
    LPs
limit order, 178, 179
Lord Jones, 115
Lotus Ventures Inc., 105
Louisiana, 78
LUMMA (Legitimate Use of
    Medicinal Marihuana Act),
    60

Luxembourg, marijuana
    possession rules in, 96

M
Maine, 78
Manitoba Harvest, 112
MAPLE Act, 60
Marihuana Tax Act (1937), 13,
    14, 15, 17, 19
marijuana, 15, 16. *See also*
    cannabis
Marijuana 1-to-3 Act of 2019, 61
Marijuana Data Collection Act,
    61
Marijuana Freedom and
    Opportunity Act, 56
Marijuana in Federally Assisted
    Housing Parity Act of 2019,
    61
Marijuana Justice Act, 61
Marijuana Opportunity
    Reinvestment and
    Expungement (MORE) Act
    (2019), 55–56
Marijuana Regulation and
    Taxation Act, 86–87
Marijuana Revenue and
    Regulation Act, 61
Marinol, 156
market order, 178
Maryland, 78
Massachusetts, 78
Matica Enterprises Inc., 106
Medical Cannabis Research Act
    of 2019, 56–57

medical marijuana, states with potential, 90–91

Medical Marijuana Research Act of 2019, 57

medical markets, states with only, 84–85

MediPharm Labs Corp., 102, 137–138

MedMen Enterprises Inc., 119, 121, 131–132

MedXtractor Corp., 106

Mellon, Andrew, 14, 16

Mellon Bank, 14

mergers and acquisitions
about, 169–170
Altria Group, Inc., 171
Anheuser-Busch InBev SA, 172
Constellation Brands, Inc., 171
Imperial Brands PLC ADR, 172
Molson Coors Beverage Company, 172–173

Mexico, legalization of cannabis in, 95

Michigan, 78, 82

micro-cap, 38

Microsoft, 31

military veterans, Federal legislation and, 57–58

Minnesota, 78

Mississippi, 78, 90

Missouri, 78, 89

MJ Freeway, 164

MJardin Group, Inc., 121

Modlin, Andrew, 132

Mojave Jane Brands Inc., 121

Molson Coors, 11

Molson Coors Beverage Company, 172–173

Montana, 78, 89

MORE Act (2019), 55–56

Mota Ventures Corp., 106

MPX International Corp., 121

MSOs (multi-state operators). See multi-state operators (MSOs)

multi-state operators (MSOs)
about, 66, 71, 117–122
honorable mentions, 131–134
recommended best, 122–129
recommended solid, 129–131

MustGrow Biologics Corp., 121

mutual funds, 181

MYM Nutraceuticals Inc., 106

N

Nabis Holdings Inc., 121

Nadler, Jerry, 56

Namaste Technologies Inc., 103

NanoSphere Health Sciences Inc., 121

NASDAQ, Canadian cannabis firms on, 66, 101

Nass Valley Gateway Ltd., 121

National Access Cannabis Corp., 103

National Highway Traffic Safety Administration, 60

National Institutes of Health (NIH), 60

National Prohibition Act (1920), 2
Nebraska, 78, 90–91
Neopharm Group, 150
Neptune Wellness Solutions Inc., 101, 102, 138–139
Netflix, 32–33
Netherlands, marijuana possession rules in, 96
Nevada, 78, 82–83
New Deal, 3
New Hampshire, 78
New Jersey, 78, 88
New Mexico, 79
New York, 49, 79, 86–87
New York Stock Exchange (NYSE), Canadian cannabis firms on, 66, 101
New Zealand, recreational use of cannabis in, 96
NewLeaf Brands Inc., 121
NeXT, 31
Next Green Wave Holdings Inc., 121
Next Step Act, 61
Nextleaf Solutions Ltd., 106
NIH (National Institutes of Health), 60
1933 Industries Inc., 120
Nixon, Richard, 17–18
non-alcoholic beverage industry, cannabis and, 22
North America
    cannabis consumption in, 96
    marijuana consumption statistics for, 95

North American Marijuana Index, 34–36, 187–188
North Bud Farms Inc., 106
North Carolina, 79
North Dakota, 79, 89–90
Novartis AG, 156
Nutritional High International Inc., 121
nylon, 14–15

O
Oklahoma, 90
Ontario, Canada, 37, 42, 68–69
opioid market, 149–150
Orchid Ventures Inc., 121
Oregon, 79, 83
Organic Flower Investments, 106
Organigram Holdings Inc., 100, 101, 102, 108–109
organized crime, growth in, 2
Orion Nutraceuticals Inc., 106
over-the-counter (OTC) market, 69–70

P
Pasha Brands Ltd., 106
Pennsylvania, 79, 87–88
PerkinElmer, Inc., 164–166
Peru, medical use of cannabis in, 96
pet product industry, cannabis and, 23
pharmaceutical industry
    about, 149–150
    cannabis and, 23
    recommended best, 150–157

PharmaCielo Ltd., 103
Pharmadrug Inc., 106
Phivada Holdings Inc., 121
Planet 13 Holdings Inc., 121
Plus Products Inc., 121
Poland, medical use of cannabis in, 96
political affiliation, legalization support and, 48–49
Predictmedix Inc., 106
Primo Nutraceuticals Inc., 121
profitability, as an alcohol industry characteristic, 9–10
Prohibition, 1–3
Pure Global Cannabis Inc., 103
Pure Sunfarms, 107

Q
quality, of product in US, 71–73
Quebec, Canada, 37, 68–69
Quinsam Capital Corp., 106

R
Rapid Dose Therapeutics Corp., 106
Ravenquest BioMed Inc., 106
Reagan, Nancy, 18
Reagan, Ronald, 18–19
real estate industry, cannabis and, 23
real estate investment trusts (REITs), 23, 122–124
recreational marijuana
　approved by ballot initiatives, 88–90
　legality of, 95–96

by state legislature, 86–88
states with, 76–84
Redfund Capital Corp., 106
Redwood Holding Group, 115
REFER Act of 2019, 61
Regulate Marijuana Like Alcohol Act, 61–62
REITs (real estate investment trusts), 23, 122–124
Removing Marijuana from Deportable Offenses Act, 62
research, Federal legislation and, 56–57
Respect States' and Citizens' Rights Act of 2019, 62
Responsibly Addressing the Marijuana Policy Gap Act of 2019, 62
revenue
　Canada LPs by 2019, 100
　US operators by, 118–119
Revive Therapeutics Ltd., 106
Rhode Island, 79
RISE Life Science Corp., 121
RMMI Corp., 106
Rockshield Capital Corp., 106
Roosevelt, Franklin D., 3, 6
Root, Al
　"What Alcohol Stocks During Prohibition Say About Marijuana Stocks Today", 6
Rubicon Organics Inc., 106

S
SAFE Act (2019), 53–54
Sanders, Bernie, 56

Sandoz, 156
SBA (Small Business Administration), 60
Schedule I drugs, 17, 18
Schedule V drugs, 17
Schumer, Chuck, 56
The Scotts Miracle-Gro Company, 167–168
Second Amendment Protection Act, 62
Second Chance for Students Act, 62
Secure and Fair Enforcement Act (SAFE) (2019), 53–54
sell stop order, 178
Sensible Business Tax Equity Act of 2019, 62
short interest, 39
short selling, 37–39
Sire Bioscience Inc., 106
Sixteenth Amendment, of the Constitution, 2
SLANG Worldwide Inc., 122
Small Business Administration (SBA), 60
small cap, 38
smoking hash, 14
SOL Global Investments Corp., 122
South Africa, legalization of cannabis in, 95
South America, medical use of cannabis in, 96
South Carolina, 79
South Dakota, 79, 88–89

SpeakEasy Cannabis Club Ltd., 106
Sproutly Canada Inc., 106
State Cannabis Commerce Act, 62
states
  about, 75–76, 79
  Alabama, 78, 91
  Alaska, 78
  Arizona, 78, 85
  Arkansas, 78, 89
  California, 45–46, 71–72, 78, 80–81
  Colorado, 46, 72–73, 76–80, 78
  Connecticut, 78, 87
  with current recreational cannabis sales, 76–84
  Delaware, 78, 87
  District of Columbia, 78
  Florida, 78, 84–85
  Georgia, 78
  Hawaii, 78
  Idaho, 78, 90
  Illinois, 49, 78, 81–82
  Iowa, 78
  Kansas, 78
  Kentucky, 78, 91
  Louisiana, 78
  Maine, 78
  Maryland, 78
  Massachusetts, 78
  with medical markets only, 84–85
  Michigan, 78, 82
  Minnesota, 78

states (*continued*)
Mississippi, 78, 90
Missouri, 78, 89
Montana, 78, 89
Nebraska, 78, 90–91
Nevada, 78, 82–83
New Hampshire, 78
New Jersey, 78, 88
New Mexico, 79
New York, 49, 79, 86–87
North Carolina, 79
North Dakota, 79, 89–90
Ohio, 79
Oklahoma, 79, 90
Oregon, 79, 83
pending new cannabis
    reform, 86–91
Pennsylvania, 79, 87–88
with potential new
    legislation, 86
Rhode Island, 79
South Carolina, 79
South Dakota, 79, 88–89
Tennessee, 79
Texas, 79
Utah, 79
Vermont, 79
Virginia, 79
Washington, 79, 84
West Virginia, 79
Wisconsin, 79
Wyoming, 79
STATES Act, 55
Stem Holdings Inc., 122
StillCanna Inc., 106
stock dilution, 40

stock loan fee, 39
stock market crash (1929), 2
stop order, 178
Strengthening the Tenth
    Amendment Through
    Entrusting States (STATES)
    Act, 55
Sugarbud Craft Growers Corp.,
    103
Sundial Growers Inc., 100, 101
Sunniva Inc., 122
suppliers, recommended stocks,
    159–168
The Supreme Cannabis
    Company, 100, 102
"Survive and Thrive"
    environment, 98
Switzerland, medical use of
    cannabis in, 96

T
Tennessee, 79
Terrace Global Inc., 103
Terranueva Corp., 106
TerrAscend Corp., 106
Tetra Bio-Pharma Inc., 103
Texas, 79
Thailand, medical use of
    cannabis in, 96
THC (delta-9-
    tetrahydrocanabinol), 23, 24
THC Biomed Intl Ltd., 106
Thermo Fisher Scientific Inc.,
    166–167
Tidal Royalty Corp., 122
Tilray Inc., 100, 101, 112–113

TILT Holdings Inc., 122
The Tinley Beverage Company
    Inc., 122
tobacco industry
    cannabis and, 23
    growth in, 15
    profitability of, 22
    statistics on, 4
Top Strike Resources Corp., 122
Toronto Stock Exchange (TSX),
    Canadian cannabis firms on,
    66, 101, 102
trade orders, 178
Transcanna Holdings Inc., 122
Tree of Knowledge
    International, 122
Tribal Marijuana Sovereignty
    Act of 2019, 63
Trichome Financial Corp., 106
True Leaf Brands Inc., 106
Trulieve Cannabis Corp., 118,
    122, 127–129
Trump, Donald, 57
TSX Venture Exchange (TSXV),
    66, 102–103
tuberculosis sclerosis complex,
    150
Twenty-First Amendment, to
    the Constitution, 1, 3, 6

U
United States
    banking in, 70
    cannabis stock in, 42–43
    compared with Canada,
        65–74

legalization in, 69–70
market size in, 69
multi-state operators (MSOs)
    in, 69–70, 117–134
product quality in, 71–73
tax rates in, 70–71
Uruguay, legalization of
    cannabis in, 36, 95
Utah, 79

V
VA Medicinal Cannabis
    Research Act of 2019, 63
VA Survey of Cannabis Use Act,
    63
Valens GroWorks Corp., 103,
    136–137
vaping, 39
Ventura Cannabis and
    Wellness, 122
Veritas Pharma Inc., 106
Vermont, 79
vertical integration, 71
veterans, military, Federal
    legislation and, 57–58
Veterans Affairs bills, 62–63
Veterans Cannabis Use for Safe
    Healing Act, 63
Veteran's Equal Access Act,
    57–58
Veteran's Medical Marijuana
    Safe Harbor Act, 58
Viacom, 32
Vibe Bioscience Ltd., 122

Village Farms International
   Inc., 100, 101, 107–108
Vinergy Cannabis Capital Inc.,
   106
Vireo Health International Inc.,
   122
Virginia, 79
VIVO Cannabis Inc., 100, 102
Vodis Pharmaceuticals Inc., 106
volatility
   about, 29
   Amazon and, 30
   Apple and, 31–32
   cannabis stocks and, 33–43
   Netflix and, 32–33
Volstead Act (1920), 2

W
"War on Drugs", 18–19
Warren, Elizabeth, 55, 56
Washington, 79, 84
Washington, George, 13
WeedMD Inc., 103
Weekend Unlimited Industries
   Inc., 122
wellness industry, cannabis
   and, 23

West Virginia, 79
"What Alcohol Stocks During
   Prohibition Say About
   Marijuana Stocks Today"
   (Root), 6
Whittle, Brian, 151
Wildflower Brands Inc., 122
Willow Biosciences Inc., 102
Wisconsin, 79
Wolf, Tom, 88
World Class Extractions Inc.,
   122
Wozniak, Steve, 31
Wyoming, 79

X
XPhyto Therapeutics Corp., 106

Y
The Yield Growth Corp., 122

Z
Zenabis Global Inc., 102
Zygel, 153–154
Zynerba Pharmaceuticals, Inc.,
   152–154